IMPROVING FOOD SECURITY

To dedicated rural development managers in every country

IMPROVING FOOD SECURITY

A guide for rural development managers

MICHAEL HUBBARD

INTERMEDIATE TECHNOLOGY PUBLICATIONS 1995

Intermediate Technology Publications Ltd
103–105 Southampton Row, London WC1B 4HH, UK

© Intermediate Technology Publications 1995

A CIP record for this book is available from
the British Library

ISBN 1 85339 311 8

Typeset by Dorwyn Ltd, Rowlands Castle, Hants
Printed in the UK by BPC Wheatons, Exeter

Contents

Preface	vii
1. PLIGHT AND POWER OF THE RURAL MANAGER	1
The person in the middle	1
What the rural manager needs to know about food security	2
2. ASSESSING FOOD SECURITY IN THE LOCALITY	7
Local food security and nutrition	7
Carrying out a local food security and nutrition audit	12
A local food security strategy	18
Summary	21
3. NUTRITION, HEALTH AND DISEASE	22
Nutrition priorities in rural areas	23
Finding out whether there is a nutrition problem in the area	26
Designing programmes to improve nutrition	33
Summary	38
4. FOOD SUPPLIES AND PRICES	39
State and market	39
Techniques for finding out how well local food markets work	41
What can be done to overcome problems	50
Summary	61
5. CREATING INCOMES AND EMPLOYMENT	63
The changing rural employment problem	63
Why government and NGOs should be involved in trying to raise and maintain people's incomes	63
Indirect measures: creating an environment that fosters productive employment for the poor	65
Direct measures to raise incomes	68
Summary	89

6. WATER — 90
The rural water management problem — 90
Potential benefits of improved water supplies — 91
Government–village partnership in water management — 91
Government's role in building sustained self-help in water management — 93
Key food security issues involving water — 94
Summary — 97

7. LIVESTOCK — 99
Managing the local livestock sector during a drought — 99
Managing livestock development to promote food security: Dos and Don'ts — 104
Summary — 107

8. FINANCE FOR LOCAL FOOD SECURITY — 109
Assessing the local financial system as it affects the poor — 110
Improving the local financial system for the poor — 113
Improving project funding — 116
Summary — 118

9. GOVERNMENT–NGO CO-OPERATION — 120
The nature of NGOs — 120
NGO dilemmas — 121
Working with local NGOs — 122
Strengths and weaknesses of national and foreign NGOs — 122
NGOs and food security — 124
Summary — 125

10. PREPAREDNESS FOR FAMINE PREVENTION — 127
The basis for disaster preparedness — 128
Essential disaster preparedness measures: national and local — 130
Making local preparedness administration more effective under adverse circumstances — 137

Appendix I: Rapid and participatory appraisal tools — 139
Appendix II: Kenya's Turkana District drought preparedness plan — 142

Glossary of food security terms — 145
Notes — 147
References — 149

Preface

This book is for rural development managers, whether in government or voluntary organizations, who are struggling to improve nutrition and reduce poverty in the local area for which they are responsible. It is a source book of issues and lessons from experience. I was inspired to write the book by working with some exceptionally able rural managers who manage to achieve much with very little. The focus is on local food security since it links priorities for improvement of nutrition, incomes and markets for food and essentials. The bias of the book is strongly towards participative investigations, decisions and management.

The meanings of food security and nutrition are clarified first, followed by suggestions on how to assess food security and nutrition problems quickly and participatively, and how to work out a local strategy for reducing them. Attention then turns to improving the local markets for health services, food, employment, water, livestock and finance, which are often critical for food security and nutrition. Finally, important managerial issues of co-operation between government and non-government organizations (NGOs) and local preparedness for famine prevention are discussed.

In many parts of the world, food insecurity and nutritional risk is often greater for females than for males, in infancy, in parenthood (particularly during pregnancy, nursing and as single parents), and in old age. Further, women are usually the key decision-makers in child nutrition. Therefore a substantial part of the challenge in improving household food security involves raising the incomes and education of disadvantaged women. This theme is interwoven through the book, particularly in Chapters 2, 3 and 5.

Many individuals and organizations have contributed material, ideas and comment. Among them are Christian Aid, ILO, Oxfam, NORAD, SIDA, SOS Sahel, Tear Fund, Tools for Self-Reliance, Unicef and USAID, who all discussed with me how their activities relate to food security priorities. Roy Behnke, Deryke Belshaw, Catherine Butcher, Barbara Harriss-White and Andrew Shepherd commented on drafts of individual chapters, as did seminar groups at Makerere University, Uganda, and the Development Studies Association conference 1993 at the University of Sussex. Ann Bolstridge typed, reformated and printed numerous drafts. Liz Paren contributed ideas, encouragement and remarkable editorial patience.

Richard Luc Hubbard provided cheerful encouragement. Carmen To deserves special thanks for typing chapters, overhauling the presentation of the entire manuscript and for her constant, loving support. The usual disclaimers apply.

Permission from Lynne Reinner publishers, to quote extracts from Jeremy Swift's description (1989) of the Turkana District drought preparedness plan, is gratefully acknowledged.

CHAPTER 1
Plight and Power of the Rural Manager

This chapter shows how and why local food security may be a useful policy focus in a rural area where there is extreme poverty. It looks first at the power and limitations of the rural manager's position, whether in government or in a non-governmental organization (NGO), and follows that with questions and answers about the nature and purpose of a food security approach.

The person in the middle

The rural manager is the person in the middle, an official with much power and no power – someone with great immediate influence over local decisions and virtually none over wider decisions; someone who commands few resources directly but who is meant to bring many resources together; who may be the arm of central government or NGO headquarters, but is also answerable to local leaders and communities. The rural manager is the person between what many see as the modern and the traditional worlds, working with people whose culture may be quite different from his or her own, in religion, marriage practices, food, and even language; a culture which may seem, especially after a difficult day, to have distasteful, anti-developmental attitudes – to women, perhaps, or to educating children. The rural manager is also the person between the 'development experts' from the capital, consultants and politicians – each with their own agenda – and the difficult reality on the ground; between the traditional leadership of chiefs and headmen (often those who hold the real power locally) and the modern, democratic system of local councils, which, in the worst cases, may hardly function at all, but with which the local manager must work. At the most frustrating times, the manager may be tempted to push and to force, but knows at heart that forcing ultimately brings non-cooperation; that patience and consultation are the way forward.

Above all, the rural government manager is the person in the middle co-ordinating public sector activities locally – even if some line ministries do not want to be co-ordinated – in improving infrastructure, health, education, law and order, price stability, and for co-ordinating relief in times of stress, e.g. droughts, floods. Current changes in the public service are putting further pressure on the public manager, as taxpayers demand less bureaucracy but more efficient and effective services, accountable and responsive to community needs (Wallis 1989).

With regard to rural development, the manager, whether in government or NGO, faces an increasing clamour from academics and politicians to be more in touch with the ordinary people, more participative and more professional. Robert Chambers has thrown down the challenge to rural administrators to develop a 'new professionalism' (Chambers 1993).

What the rural manager needs to know about food security

What does the already overburdened, under-resourced rural manager need to know about food security – a term he or she may not have heard of, but has gathered means people having enough to eat? Here is some basic information, put in the form of a dialogue; perhaps it is best to imagine this conversation taking place above the rattling metallic din of a vehicle on a bad rural road:

Does food security simply mean people having enough to eat?

It means people being able to get the food they need to be healthy and active, wherever they get it from and however it is provided. It also means people being confident that adequate food will be available at all times.

Then food security depends on people being able to get the food they need?

Yes, and for adults or household units that depends on the income they receive, the savings and other assets they have, and what the cost of food is; for small children that depends also on the food they are given.

So a household or individuals within a household can lack food security?

Yes, it is useful to focus on household food security, since the household is the basic earning and decision-making unit on which the most nutritionally vulnerable people (i.e. infants and small children, pregnant and nursing women) depend. But it is also useful to consider the food security of individual persons in the household, in order to help to improve food quality and distribution within the household.

Are female members of households likely to be more food insecure than males?

This is often the case. In regions of the world where, on average, infant mortality of females is higher than males (south Asia, east Asia, Middle East), female infant malnutrition rates are also often higher, suggesting that less care is often given to female babies. The greater nutritional needs of pregnant and nursing mothers, their dependence on the earnings of others, the frequent lack among female single parents of dependable partners, combine to increase their vulnerability.

Can a country lack food security?

In the same way as a household, a country is vulnerable to food insecurity if there is a risk that food supplies in the country may fall below requirements without the means of bringing in additional food. The reason may be lack of foreign exchange or credit to pay for imports but usually is the result of logistical problems: lack of trucks, shipping, port handling facilities, or blockades in times of war. Crises of national food security are usually started by widespread losses of household food security; for example, following crop failures. Logistical and distributional failures are at the centre of national food security crises, as causes both of inadequate national food security and of inability to relieve household food insecurity even when there is sufficient food available in the country to do so. The way forward to better national food security is improved household food security and improved market infrastructure.

So household food insecurity can exist even where there is national food security?

This is frequently the case: that some households do not have the means to acquire enough food even where it is available, resulting in malnutrition within the household.

What is the difference between food security and nutrition?

A person's nutrition depends on the nutrients they absorb into their bloodstream. So nutrition depends both on the nutritional value and quantity of food people eat and on whether their digestive systems are able to absorb the nutrients from the food. For example, a child with vomiting and diarrhoea is not able to absorb the nutrients from the food eaten.

So malnutrition can also be present in households which are food secure?

Yes, this is not unusual. Nutritionally vulnerable individuals within the household may be food secure (i.e. receive sufficient good food) but suffer from malnutrition since nutrition depends also on a person's state of health, i.e. the nutrients their bodies are able to absorb. Poor sanitary conditions in and around the home, causing recurring diarrhoeal diseases, may be a major cause of infant and child malnutrition and mortality.

So if you cannot tell from the presence or absence of malnutrition whether the household or individual is food secure or not, how do you tell?

Since household food security is *access* by the household to sufficient food, it depends on the household commanding enough resources (productive assets, income from them, savings, ability to borrow) always to get enough food. But there is no exact measure of this. The amount of resources required, when people eat different foods and spend their resources in different ways, cannot be generalized. There is therefore no single level of income below which a household lacks food security. As a result, estimates of the number of people lacking food security are very rough and are usually based on the nutrition levels of the population; for example, the percentage of the population consuming insufficient calories for an active working life (below 90 per cent of the FAO/WHO calorie requirement) is one estimate that has been used (World Bank, 1986).

Doesn't this just amount to saying that a family lacking food security is extremely poor?

Yes, food insecurity at the household level means extreme poverty: not being sure that the family will have enough to eat if income falls, prices rise substantially, or the family increases, is the direst poverty. It has been called 'primary poverty' in the past (Hagenbuch 1958) and more recently 'food poverty' (Von Braun and Pandya-Lorch 1992).

How is household food security a useful concept then? Wouldn't it be better to focus on extreme poverty and malnutrition as the basic problems?

It is a useful concept for at least four reasons:

Firstly, expenditure on food makes up a large percentage of total expenditure of the poor.

Secondly, in rural areas access by poor households to an adequate supply of staple food may be particularly critical: an abundant supply of staple food means that the small amount of cash earned can be used for other purposes; the failure of a staple crop throws households into deficit, often with too little and uncertain cash incomes to cover the deficit.

Thirdly, food security emphasizes vulnerability, i.e. how secure people's access to food is. A household that is food insecure is vulnerable to external shocks[1] that reduce its income (e.g. drought, floods, pest attacks on crops) or that greatly raise the price of essential consumer goods. Households which are chronically food insecure (i.e. barely get enough to eat in normal times) are more vulnerable to acute food insecurity (i.e. severe lack of access to food) when hit by external shocks.

Fourthly, food security is a flexible, linking concept for analysing the food access side of the nutrition problem, the other side of it stemming from disease. Food security is adapted to different levels of aggregation (the individual, the household, the country) but focuses on the same issue in all cases: the linking of nutrition to markets (food, labour, assets such as livestock, land), to household decision-making (with regard to work and child care) and to public policy (subsidies, taxes, regulations, investments).

Food security is not a popular concern – particularly with central government. There is concern just after a drought or other disaster; but soon the focus becomes economic growth, and growth requires productive investment, not redistribution.

Productive investment and income growth are basic to food security. Where there is severe poverty, including food security considerations in investment planning helps to link that investment to the reduction of malnutrition and famine risk.

Another problem is that there is little that can be done to improve food security locally, because people's incomes, prices of food and health services are all determined from outside the locality; local governments and voluntary organizations have no control over these, and few resources of their own.

4

There may be much that can be done at little cost, by improving organization, and drawing on experience elsewhere in dealing with the same problems. The greatest resource is the communities' and individuals' own energies; the rural development manager's function is to help release these, in which participative appraisal and planning techniques play a large role. Moreover, in areas where there is any famine risk, costs put into prevention are minute compared with those of fighting famine. The benefits are immeasurable. Even without external financial support, local government and local NGOs can help as follows.

○ Increase community involvement in improving nutrition and reducing disease, through working with local groups, particularly women's groups. Activities can include keeping kitchen utensils cleaner, weighing and measuring babies on a community basis in order to monitor their progress, spreading local best practice in vegetable growing, weaning, food preparation and use.
○ Increase community involvement in sustainable use of common resources by collecting (e.g. through local school projects) and sharing information on changes in rivers, wetlands, grazing lands, lakes, wildlife and forests, and exploring and promoting local ideas regarding how they can best be managed.
○ Remove 'red tape' (e.g. unnecessary licences or permits for retailing, milling and transporting) which raises local food prices, reduces producer prices and reduces markets for local produce.

With relatively little external funding there is much that local action can do to improve food security, both to relieve chronic food insecurity and prevent acute food insecurity; for example:

○ creating incomes and employment, through providing access to productive assets for the needy and labour intensive employment projects;
○ creating and protecting fall-back assets and sources of income (i.e. sources of income that the needy can fall back on during times of stress), such as managed forests, fisheries, irrigation;
○ improving the functioning of local markets for food and other essentials such as water, fuel, livestock and drugs;
○ improving and encouraging central government and NGO initiatives in the locality by providing better project planning and management;
○ encouraging community participation in reducing malnutrition.

Food security is not such a problem in fertile, food surplus rural areas. Don't government and NGOs have much more of a food security role in a high risk area?

The risks of acute food security problems (i.e. famine) are less in food surplus areas. But often chronic food security problems are greater in these areas in the form of higher levels of infant and child malnutrition, because of concentrations of poor people there, seeking work, earning little or living on very small plots of land, and with greater risk of disease. In these areas the need to provide food market security against the risks of drought, floods or civil disturbance is usually less, but greater stress may be needed on nutrition improvement.

Is food security a useful concept in reducing urban poverty?

Malnutrition caused by inadequate access to food is not confined to rural areas. Urban nutrition programmes tend to be focused on nutrition education, subsidization of food prices to the poor (e.g. via food stamps) and improving food quality. Urban markets usually function fairly well, so that food supplies are not at risk to the same extent as in many rural areas. Income generation remains as important a concern as it is in rural areas, but with a greater stress on secondary and tertiary activities.

Is there much that rural administrators can learn about promoting food security in their areas?

There is now a large body of experience accumulated in both famine prevention and reducing chronic food insecurity. Many lessons have been learned concerning better and worse ways of consulting, communicating, intervening and organizing. It is the purpose of this book to provide an overview of this experience and present it in an accessible, straightforward way, so that the rural administrator can quickly check a food security problem against the experience accumulated elsewhere in tackling such problems. There are rarely any solutions to local problems that can simply be taken from a book. But lessons from experience elsewhere can prevent the repetition of errors and provide new ideas.

The next chapter discusses how to get started in the assessment of food security in the locality.

CHAPTER 2
Assessing Food Security in the Locality

The purpose of this chapter is to assist in carrying out a quick food security audit of the area in order to identify trends of change that affect food security, to subdivide the area according to differences in local food security systems, and to outline a food security strategy for the area. The 'audit' requires few resources and relies heavily on rapid and participative techniques of gathering and analysing information, backed up by whatever data may be available on local populations, their sources of income, and their state of health. The reason for relying on rapid and participative techniques is not only that they lead to quicker (and sometimes sounder) information than questionnaire surveys, but also that they promote and facilitate communication, discussion and joint action with communities. See Appendix I for a summary of the philosophy and some techniques of rapid and participatory appraisal. By setting out a framework for understanding local food security the chapter provides an introduction to the rest of the book, each chapter of which is concerned with a particular aspect of local food security.

The chapter begins by clarifying what local food security means and how it is determined by a number of causes that are related to each other in a local food security and nutrition system. This is followed by suggestions on how to assess quickly, with community participation, the changes and differences in local food security systems and the effectiveness of government and other local community institutions in trying to improve them. There is then a discussion of ways to apply the results of the audit to designing a strategy for improving food security locally.

Local food security and nutrition

Whereas concern with *national food security* focuses on supplies of food within the country, ability to import as required and ability to distribute supplies to areas of need, concern with *local food security* focuses on the household and the individual members of households having access to sufficient food for an active and healthy life. This depends on their income, work, health (linked to nutrition) and distribution of food within the household, as well as on local food supplies and costs of other essential daily consumer items, i.e. water and fuel (assuming that in a rural area basic housing is not a major cost).

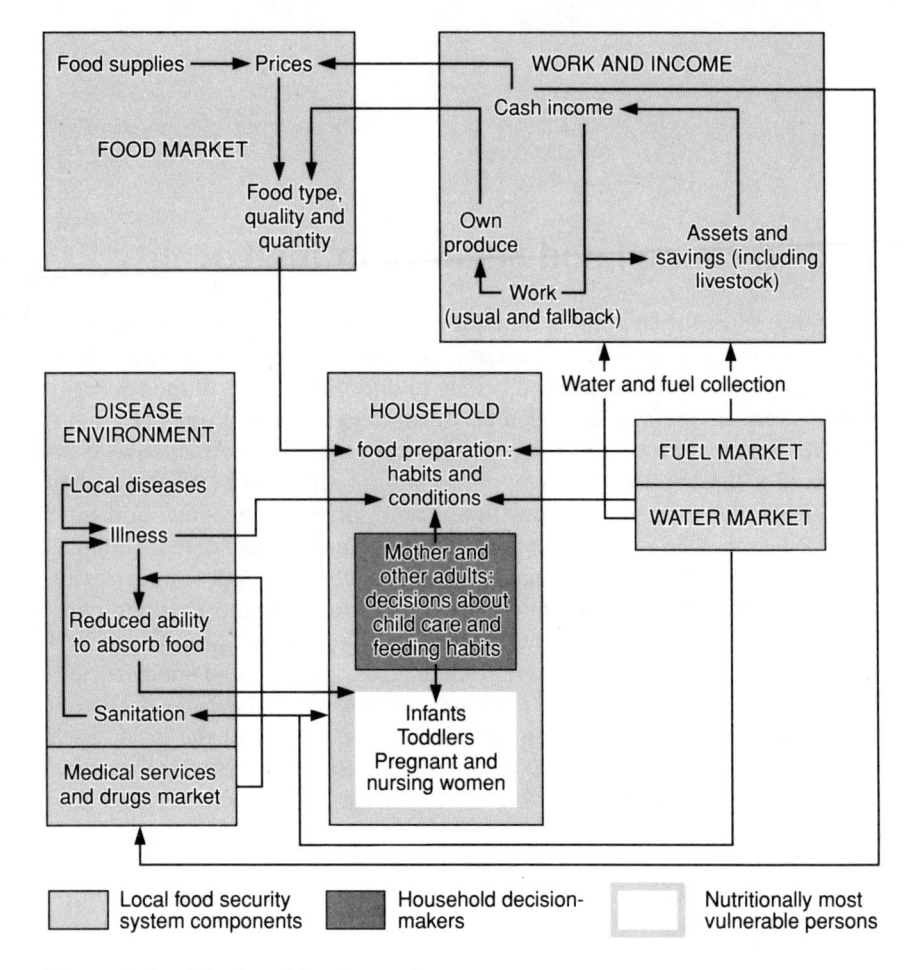

Figure 2.1 *The local food security system*

It is useful to think of local food security and nutrition as determined in a system consisting of the local food market (i.e. production, transport, storage, processing, wholesaling and retailing of food) together with the means of acquiring food, and the causes of what and how much food the vulnerable household members receive, and the nutrients they are able to absorb.

Figure 2.1 illustrates the interactive components determining local food security and nutrition: the household, its health environment, work, assets and income, and the local markets for food, water and fuel. At the centre of the system is the household, with its most nutritionally vulnerable people (infants, toddlers, pregnant and nursing women) and those who most closely determine their welfare (mothers and other adult decision-makers) through their work patterns, income, and habits of food preparation, distribution and child care. The close links between the health environment and nutrition of the most vulnerable are via local diseases and illness, sanitation, food preparation habits and conditions, and the medical services and drugs market. Work, assets and income determine the resources available – the 'exchange entitlements' to use Sen's term (Sen 1981, Dreze and Sen 1989) – to provide food, medical services and water, and who is available to look after the infants and toddlers. The food market determines food types, quality and quantities and prices to be paid, while the water and fuel markets determine the availability, prices and collection time required (which reduce time for productive work and child care), while the water market influences sanitation habits and possibilities.

It is a local *system* because the factors in the local environment that determine food security and nutrition are interlinked; they also determine, and are in turn affected by, the adjustments that people make in order to survive under conditions of stress. For example, drought causes loss of assets (especially livestock) and resort to emergency, fall-back food sources and work possibilities (especially migrant work). It may also change work and child care habits, water supplies and use, and affect the quantity, type, preparation and distribution of food among household members, and their exposure to disease.

The system is *local* because it varies from locality to locality according to work, assets and health environment, household and inter-household culture, food and water markets. Thus even within a single district or subdistrict there may be different local food security systems, though they may have some features in common.

Social relations among households by which they informally share work, lend and borrow among themselves affect local food security and nutrition. The 'social entitlements'[1] of households differ according to culture and the degree of stress upon the local community. Under great stress, for example a severe drought and impending famine, debts and obligations may be cancelled rather than extended further, as social co-operation breaks down.

In general, a local food security system works better the more that government and NGO actions locally:

- facilitate, rather than oppose the strategies of vulnerable households;
- increase the diversity of their income-earning opportunities;
- enable markets (particularly for food and livestock) to work more smoothly and to avoid major price instability in times of stress, e.g. during and after droughts;
- give a high priority to the welfare of infants and young children and to women's education;
- conserve and enhance common assets (forests, wild animals, rivers, lakes).

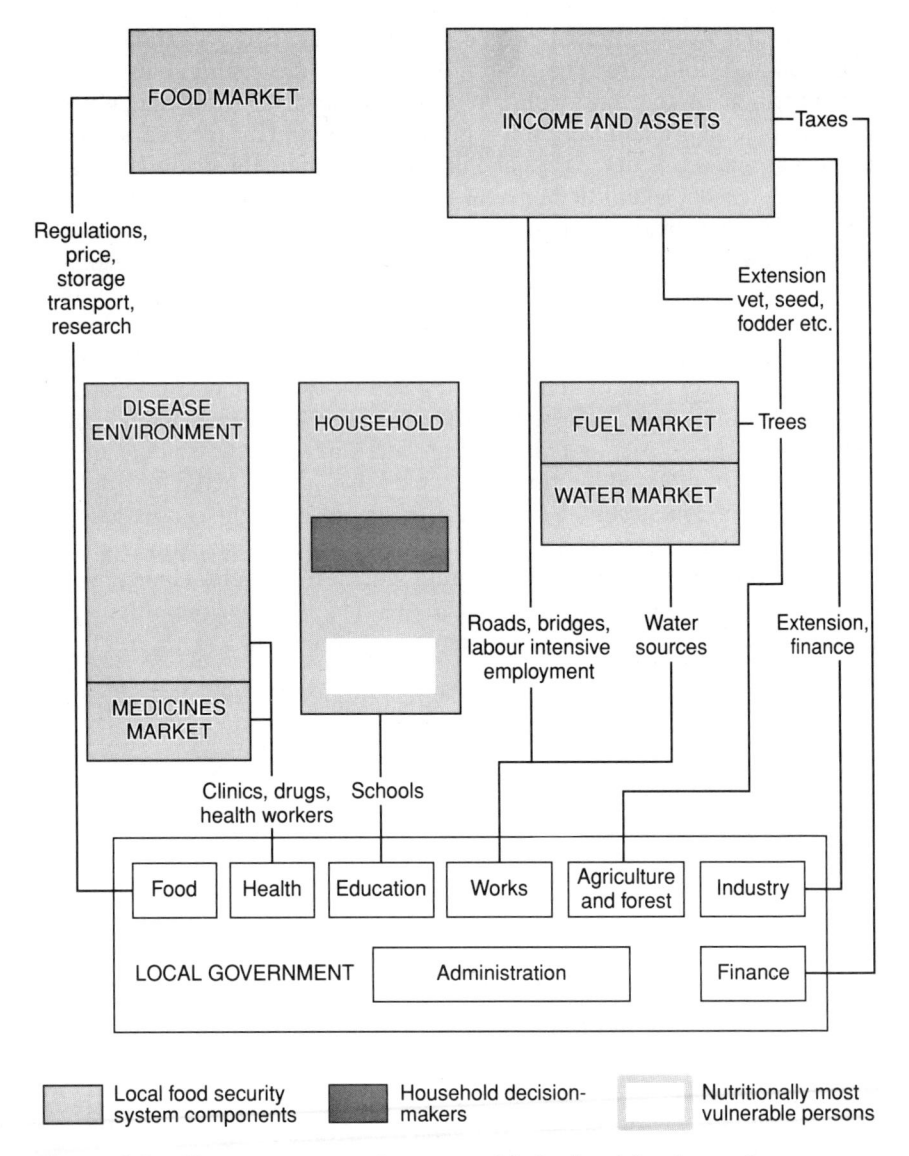

Figure 2.2 *How government interacts with the local food security system*

The role of government
Government actions affect the local food security system at a number of points, as indicated in Figure 2.2. The rectangular block at the lower part of the figure represents government, divided into a typical set of line and co-ordinating departments present at the district level. The shaded areas are the six components of the local food security system (simplified from Figure 2.1). The lines represent links between government actions and local food security

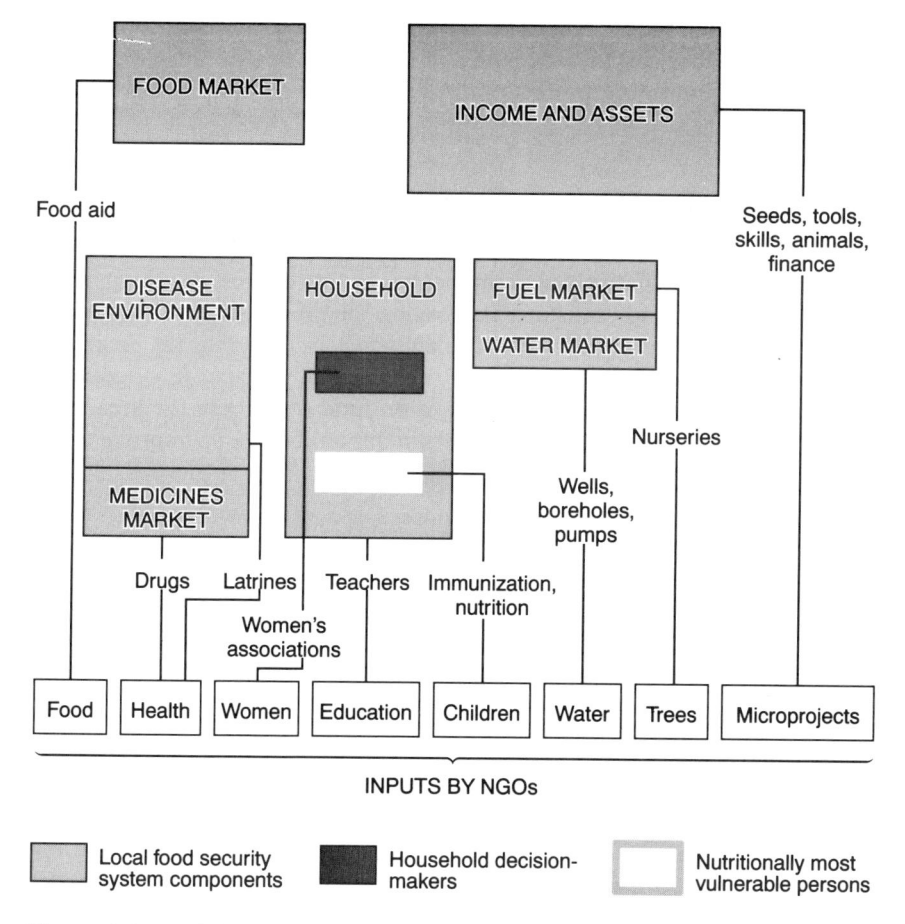

Figure 2.3 *NGOs activities and the local food security system*

systems in the form of government *investments* (e.g. roads, schools, clinics, water points), *services* (e.g. health, agricultural and veterinary extension, school teachers, maintenance of public works), *regulations* (e.g. public health, environment, food trading) and *charges* (taxes, user charges for services).

The role of NGOs
Like government, NGOs stand outside the local food security system, in a position to strengthen it through their actions. NGOs, however, generally have welfare as their primary objective whereas government's local responsibilities are not solely developmental, others being law and order, revenue or, at the most reduced level, simply being the local arm of central government. It is particularly in reduced circumstances of government that the contribution of NGOs to local food security is most critical. Figure 2.3

shows the areas of the local food security system in which NGOs commonly work and the services they provide; many are in health, education and small income-generating projects directed to the welfare of children and women.

Carrying out a local food security and nutrition audit

A quick assessment of local food security and nutrition relies on using techniques of participative appraisal combined with secondary information (available reports and statistics) to provide an overall picture of (1) the direction and nature of socio-economic change in the area, (2) local differences in food security systems, (3) the effect of the actions of government and non-government organizations on food security in the area, and (4) possible changes in actions of government and NGOs to improve their impact on food security.

1. Understanding the direction and nature of socio-economic change in the area
The purpose of identifying the main long-term, ongoing socio-economic changes in the area is to:

o understand their benefits and costs;
o identify the trends which are alterable beneficially by policy changes;
o anticipate changes and design policy accordingly.

The image of rural areas as unchanging is a false one. All rural areas (the remote and less remote, the prosperous and less prosperous) are caught up in the long-term economic and social changes associated with urbanization, population growth, increased communication and market growth. Some are gaining population – notably the more prosperous ones where there is a better chance of jobs and survival by performing petty services. Others – many small villages – are losing population, particularly in areas where water and soil are increasingly exhausted; new settlements emerge in virgin forest land and mountainous areas previously too remote, their resources of timber and soil now desperately sought for survival or to turn a short-term profit with tractors and chainsaws. But these areas are increasingly few – everywhere the last frontiers are closing, in rain forests, on mountain slopes and dry steppe land. Overall, the picture is of rapid change in land use and settlement in the rural areas of lower income countries.

These long-term changes are part of a wider pattern that includes the food economy nationally and internationally. A decreasing percentage of the population is fully employed in agriculture and people's living standards are increasingly affected by the market price of food, as fewer of them are food producers. Rural people rely increasingly on diverse sources of income including migrants' remittances, local small industries and services as well as farm production.

In general, the underlying rural trend is towards more diverse and non-agricultural sources of incomes among rural people, more reliance on trade, less on production for subsistence or on-farm storage, and more on commercial land use. Improved but congested transport and communications, and enlarged residential areas in rural towns accompany this process.

Of course in any particular locality this trend may or may not be in evidence at all, depending on whether local characteristics promote or hinder it. The process may be promoted, slowed, halted or altered by several factors including economic growth in the economy as a whole, physical features, cultural isolation, institutional and policy rigidity, population movements.

To assist in making a rapid assessment of the trend of change in the area[2] concerned, a brief checklist is presented as Box 2.1, focusing attention on general changes (population, urbanization, land use, resources and institutions) basic to any rural area, and on the features that distinguish local food security systems. Participatory appraisal will provide most of the information; see Appendix I.

2. Distinguishing local food security systems

The same participatory appraisal exercise, used with Box 2.1, will help to distinguish differences among local food security systems and changes within them. The purpose in distinguishing local food security systems is to establish priorities for improvement. Therefore the focus is on finding out which are the weakest components in food security systems.

Local food security systems differ to the extent that their components differ. The source and stability of income and of fall-back income strongly determine food security, and are accordingly the primary characteristic of the local food security system. This suggests that where farming is the main source of income, differences in local farm conditions are the main determinant of variations among local food security systems; these in turn are strongly determined by rainfall, soil type, ground and surface water availability. For this reason, the obvious divisions to check for first in predominantly farming areas are the different *rainfall catchment areas* of the district, since local variations in farming systems often conform to catchment areas, with their boundaries of high ground and valleys centred on rivers and major streams.

Other components of local food security systems also differ, as in the case of variations in the disease-nutrition synergy: staple foods, sanitary habits, housing conditions, prevalence of fly- or water-borne diseases, costs of and access to water and fuel. In general, local differences among food security systems are greater in more remote and less developed areas. The less remote, the more developed and integrated the rural area, the more

> **Box 2.1** *Features of local socio-economic change and local food security systems: a brief checklist of questions and issues*
>
> Features of local socio-economic change:
>
> *Population:*
> - Is the area losing or gaining population?
> - Is the composition of the population changing, i.e. does it consist increasingly of young people or of old people?
>
> *Urbanization:*
> - Do more and more of the population of the area live in the towns?
> - Are ordinary people increasingly dependent on non-farm employment?
>
> *Land use:*
> - Is farm land used increasingly intensively, i.e. is there more vacant land, or land left fallow?
> - Is land used increasingly for crops and less for pasture?
> - Is the area of natural forest receding?
> - Do ordinary people have less or more access to common land, fishing grounds and forest?
>
> *Infrastructure:*
> - Are roads, water supplies, communication facilities, education and training facilities, health care facilities, better or worse than ten years ago?
>
> Features of local food security systems and changes within them, with particular regard to poorer households:
>
> *Nature of the household and decision-making:*
> - Household size, number and spacing of children
> - Proportion of female-headed households
> - Education level of mothers
> - Food preparation and distribution in the household
> - Child care: breastfeeding, weaning age and weaning food, child minding, school attendance.
>
> *How households earn their living:*
> - Proportion of food requirements produced by the household itself (i.e. change in reliance on food markets)
> - Type of farming practised

similar the food security systems tend to be. The risk of acute food insecurity, following drought, floods or civil disturbance, also tends to be higher in remote, less developed areas, further away from the main population centres[3].

3. Are some people in the locality particularly at risk?
Within any local area, there are some people more at risk than others. Ethnic minorities, or those discriminated against by caste or religion, are

- o Reliance on farm/non-farm work
- o Mother's employment
- o Reliance on local/migrant income
- o Incomes (measured in purchasing power over local consumer goods).

The costs that households face in the most important markets affecting food security: increases in prices, stability of prices and sources

- o Food (seasonal fluctuations; processing costs)
- o Water
- o Fuel
- o Livestock
- o Medical.

Nutrition and the disease environment:

- o Prevalence of malnutrition among children under five years
- o Prevalence of major diseases related to nutrition, particularly among children under five years of age, such as malaria, measles, diarrhoea and vomiting, kwashiorkor, marasmus
- o Domestic conditions of sanitation and cleanliness in food preparation and storage.

The institutional environment:

- o Presence and effectiveness of government agencies and NGOs working in health, income generation and food supply and distribution.

Sources of information:
Participatory sources: See Appendix I on participatory appraisal methods.
  Interviews, individually with key informants (key health personnel, community and women's leaders, teachers, farmers) and group interviews; carrying out exercises such as constructing *sketch maps* (showing the local area and the major physical changes that have occurred in it, e.g. in settlement, forest, common land), and *ranking* (for preferences and costs), will probably be the main sources of information.
Documentary sources:

- o *Census statistics* where available. They may be difficult to find, out of date and of doubtful accuracy; but some estimates may be available of changes over time in overall population in local administrative areas and towns, and of land productivity for the main crops.
- o Local *hospital and clinic records* of the diseases and of the causes of mortality among those admitted.

often among the local poor. In many parts of the world, food insecurity and nutritional risk of females is often higher than that of males. They are particularly vulnerable in infancy, pregnancy, lactation and old age. Female headed households are also often at more risk of poverty than those in which both parents are present. Marriage practices, child rearing practices and greater female longevity all make for a higher proportion of female single parents, and single old people, than male.

Box 2.2 *Typical food security system features, problems and interventions*

Remote areas: undeveloped infrastructure, scattered population

Component	Typical features	Typical food security problems	Typical interventions
Income	Own farming, herding, gathering, transfers, wage employment only seasonal and scattered	Low incomes, high risk: vulnerable to drought and disturbance, seasonal	Cheaper agric. inputs, higher producer prices, better agric. techniques, more agric. income opportunities, skills training
Fall-back incomes	Gathering, charcoal making, migration, credit, assets sale	Dwindling common resources, information lack, costly transport, disease risk, poor credit risk	Drought reserves, afforestation, assisted migration, emergency credit, food/cash for work, food distribution, early warning
Markets: ○ Food ○ Livestock ○ Cash crops	Small, scattered, separated by high transport costs	Unstable	Improved roads, local food storage, fodder reserves, food/animal swaps, market places, handling facilities, deregulation of trade
○ Medical	Private, informal, poorly functioning clinics	Poor care, misused drugs	Essential drugs, packs, village health workers
○ Water and fuel	Scattered sources	Easily depleted, high time cost	Creating renewable, rechargeable, convenient sources

Differences between local food security systems usually stem from differences in the source of income (e.g. pastoral farming, river flood cultivation) and in the disease environment (e.g. sanitation). By contrast, the most vulnerable households in different localities are often similar in being dependent upon gifts, occasional casual work and help from family and neighbours.

Identifying the very poorest and most vulnerable is critical for relief purposes, as discussed on page 20 under 'Targeting'. This can be done by

Component	Typical features	Typical food security problems	Typical interventions
Disease–nutrition links	Micronutrient deficiencies in staples, e.g. vitamins and iron, seasonal lacks, poor weaning, poor food hygiene	Unvaried diet, chronic malnutrition, high diarrhoea and vomiting risk, stunting, high infection susceptibility	Local production of fruit and vegetables, better food storage, village-based mother and child care, nutrition and hygiene education programmes
Accessible areas: more developed infrastructure, denser population			
Incomes	Wage employment and self-employment on farms, in petty manufacturing and services	Low incomes	Raising productivity, non-agric. income generation, asset and skill
Fall-back incomes	Petty services, casual labour, welfare, credit, begging	Over traded, very limited welfare coverage	Targeted welfare by NGOs
Markets: ○ Food ○ Livestock ○ Cash crops ○ Housing	Relatively large and stable	Prices of consumables, housing	Infrastructure improvement and price assistance
○ Medical	More state care, private drugs provision	Poor care, misused drugs, high cost of hospitals	Essential drugs packs, aid to hospitals
○ Water and fuel	More stand-pipes, charcoal, electricity	Costs, reliability, depletion of forests	Water and fuel infrastructure
Disease–nutrition links	Poor weaning, poor food hygiene	High diarrhoea and vomiting risk, stunting, high infection susceptibility	Mother and child programmes, nutrition and hygiene education, housing and drainage

assessing households' incomes, as has been widely carried out in India under the IRDP programme, in order to estimate the increase in income that a household needs to cross the poverty line. But this process is time consuming, often inaccurate, and unnecessary for relief purposes. Who the most vulnerable households are is usually well known in the local community. Therefore rapid and participatory appraisal techniques (such as wealth ranking and small group interviews) are appropriate, both to identify the most needy and to involve the local community in the process.

4. Assessing the effectiveness of the interventions of government and NGOs

Few interventions (i.e. policies, programmes and projects of government, parastatals and NGOs) are designed directly to improve food security, but many affect the local food security system.

Box 2.2 summarizes some frequently encountered features, problems and interventions by government and NGOs in rural food security systems. Rural areas differ of course in many ways. To take some account of this, Box 2.2 illustrates one difference, that between remote areas, with lower population density and less developed infrastructure, and accessible rural areas with denser population, more developed infrastructure and usually greater proximity to major population centres. Some typical features, problems and policy interventions in the two tend to be similar (e.g. low incomes, links between disease and nutrition, the need to raise skills) while others may differ (e.g. functioning of markets, sources and availability of water and fuel, fall-back incomes).

With the aid of Box 2.2, used as a checklist of components and issues, a quick audit of the main features and problems of local food security systems can be made. This in turn provides a basis for assessing the impact of activities of government and NGOs as they affect local food security. Rapid and participatory appraisal techniques are recommended for gathering information for the audit. Focus group interviews, key informant interviews, participatory diagramming, and scoring and ranking alternatives are some of the techniques which can be used (see Appendix I for more). Besides providing information they also bring local development managers into close contact with the community, conveying their enthusiasms, dislikes, ways of approaching issues and suggested solutions.

A local food security strategy

The rough picture that emerges of government and NGO interventions as they affect local food security systems will probably indicate that a deliberate strategy to improve food security in the area is not being followed: few, if any, governments or NGOs have adopted explicit local food security strategies, since their overt development priorities are usually in infrastructure and improvement of local services (education, water, sewerage, health, produce markets, refuse disposal, housing) and production. But whether or not government or NGOs have or want an explicit food security strategy, carrying out the local food security audit assesses the effect of their actions on the local food security system and the direction of change required if they are to improve local food security. In Chapter 8 some simple techniques are suggested for building food security considerations into routine local project planning.

Priorities
Setting a strategy means selecting priorities for change. The benefits of having a food security strategy for the district, however rough and ready, are that it provides:

- an indication of which improvements are important and which are less important for better food security;
- a basis for checking more easily the food security implications of local development projects;
- an incentive to review policy and to improve local food security data;
- a practical means of turning development policy and projects towards women's needs (since mother and child are at the centre of food security) and environmental recovery (since local environmental deterioration usually undermines the incomes of the food insecure most).

Designing the strategy
This requires focusing on:

- the weakest components in local food security systems;
- how effective government and NGO interventions are with regard to those components;
- improved or new interventions with regard to those components.

Designing a strategy also requires time, commitment and participation of all parties involved. A useful technique to assist in strategy design is the 'ZOPP', promoted by the German NGO, GTZ. It provides a framework for identifying problems, restating these as objectives, and then assessing alternative actions to see which will most effectively attain the objectives. Using it effectively requires an experienced trainer (see Boehm 1988, 1992).

Principal issues
The principal issues in designing a local food security strategy are, firstly, whether there is a risk of acute food insecurity (i.e. famine) in the locality and, secondly, whether interventions can and should be targeted to the most needy.

Famine risk
Where there is famine risk preparedness arrangements are essential, since the costs of famine (human, social, financial, environmental) are intolerable, while the means of preventing famine are straightforward to administer (see Chapter 10). In districts or subdistricts with a high risk of acute food insecurity, governments and NGOs need and often have, explicit and specific famine prevention strategies. These emphasize either direct delivery of food supplementation, targeted to a greater or lesser extent to those most in need, or – in better organized states – income supplementing, labour intensive works programmes (see Chapter 4).

Targeting
Some types of assistance can be targeted to needy households by 'self-targeting' (public works employment, subsidies to inferior foods, i.e. those consumed mainly by the poor, feeding of undernourished infants at clinics), some by direct delivery to households (assets, including rations). Some can only be targeted to particular localities. Box 2.3 summarizes the targeting possibilities of interventions in food security systems.

Targeting of assistance to households is usually the preferred form since it requires less of the resource to be distributed and does not flood markets, which is a frequent complaint about distributed food aid. But under conditions of stress (e.g. famine) targeting by direct delivery of food to the most needy households may be particularly difficult, as experience in recent droughts and famines in Africa indicates, because every household may regard itself as needy. Since targeting by direct delivery to households is administratively intensive, 'self-targeting' (in which beneficiaries select themselves, as in the case of people presenting themselves for labour intensive work) is the most easily administered form. Two forms of self-targeting (labour intensive employment and

Box 2.3 *Targeting possibilities for interventions in the food security and nutrition system*

	Households self-targeted	Direct delivery to households	Targeting locality
INCOMES			
Assets (inc. rations)		*	
Emergency incomes (i.e. public works)	*		
MARKETS			
Subsidies to inferior foods	*		
Livestock			*
Cash crops			*
Water			*
Fuel			*
Medicines			*
DISEASE–NUTRITION LINKS			
Infant feeding at clinics	*		
Nutrition education			*
Sanitation			*

feeding undernourished infants at health posts) can be particularly effective in times of stress.

Summary

1. The food security and nutrition of households depend on the size and stability of their income, the costs they face for essentials (food, water, fuel), the disease and medical environment surrounding them, and child care and feeding practices within the household. These are loosely linked together in a local *food security system*: the economic and social means of survival for poorer people locally (illustrated in Figure 2.1). It may serve them well at some times, less well at others. It varies from one area to another; it is an open and changing system, just as local economies are open and changing.
2. An assessment of local food security and nutrition relies on using techniques of rapid and participative appraisal combined with secondary information (available written reports and statistics) to provide an overall picture of (i) the direction and nature of socio-economic change in the area, (ii) local differences in food security systems, (iii) the effect of the actions of government and NGOs on food security in the area, and (iv) possible changes in actions of government and NGOs to improve their impact on food security.
3. Devising a local food security strategy has several advantages, the main one being that it sets in process a continuing dicussion on key problems, objectives and on the effectiveness of local institutions, both government and non-government. A local food security strategy is essential where there is famine risk.

CHAPTER 3
Nutrition, Health and Disease

Poor nutrition is the most common cause of the following health problems. In children:

○ *failure of a child to grow or gain weight normally*
○ *slowness in walking, talking or thinking*
○ *swollen bellies, thin arms and legs*
○ *sadness, lack of energy*
○ *swelling of feet, face and hands, often with sores or marks on the skin*
○ *thinning or loss of hair, or loss of its colour or shine*
○ *dryness of eyes, blindness.*

In anyone:

○ *weakness and tiredness*
○ *loss of appetite*
○ *anemia*
○ *sores in the corner of the mouth*
○ *painful or sore tongue*
○ *'burning' or numbness of feet.*

(Werner 1980)

At the World Food Conference in 1974, there was optimism that hunger would be eliminated within a decade. Twenty years later that goal is far from being achieved, although in several developing countries much progress has been made (Unicef 1992, World Bank 1992). The harsh economic conditions of the 1980s were most difficult for the poorest countries where shortages of finance have forced concerns with welfare back from the broader front of 'basic needs' provision to protecting nutrition, the last line of defence in welfare. Finance has been increasingly on a project basis and dependent on aid inputs. One compensation has been the experience gained in designing and managing programmes to improve nutrition under adverse circumstances. This in itself is grounds for optimism – there is increasing confidence that the high levels of under-five mortality and malnutrition can be greatly reduced at low expense, as communities adopt a child survival orientation. Increasingly influential is the approach of Unicef and WHO through promotion of:

- prolonged breastfeeding (to transmit some immune protection from mother to child, to reduce diarrhoeal diseases and increase child spacing);
- oral rehydration salts (ORS) to enable infants to survive and recover from diarrhoea and vomiting;
- child immunization against the six killer infectious diseases (tuberculosis, measles, diphtheria, tetanus, polio, whooping cough);
- growth monitoring of infants and children;
- access to clean water (through protecting springs, wells and boreholes, and filtering using simple village-made water filters: an ordinary pot with a plug at the base in which are layered pebbles at the bottom, then coarse sand, broken charcoal and fine sand on top);
- sanitation (the 'VIP' pit latrine);
- cleanliness in food preparation and handling (e.g. simple drying racks for utensils).[1]

The WHO/Unicef Nutrition Support Programme in Iringa, Tanzania (see Box 3.1), and the door-to-door basic health assistance project in Ceara state, north-eastern Brazil[2], are strikingly successful examples of this approach.

Nutrition priorities in rural areas

Nutrition and health are integral to each other
Undernourishment is linked to ill-health as both cause and effect – it increases susceptibility to disease and limits recuperative capacity. Ill-health in turn causes lower absorption of nutrients, particularly in infants who are the most vulnerable to nutrition deficiencies and disease.

The principal nutrition problem is usually undernourishment
Undernourishment means too few calories, so that proteins get used by the body to provide energy instead of building the body. While children under five years and pregnant and nursing mothers are the most vulnerable, undernourishment of adults in general threatens the health of their dependants. Undernourishment is caused either by lack of food or by the inability of the body to absorb the nutrients it takes in, owing to disease. Furthermore, if the food is lacking in minerals, vitamins and key trace elements, this will itself reduce resistance to disease. The worst diets in rural areas are heavily carbohydrate based with few sources of protein. Three common nutrient deficiencies in such diets are:

- insufficient *iron and folic acid*, causing anaemia
- insufficient *vitamin A*, causing nightblindness and even permanent blindness, and increasing susceptibility to respiratory and diarrhoeal diseases

○ insufficient *iodine*, causing goitre, where there is too little iodine in the local soil.

All three are best remedied by increasing fresh vegetables, fruit, nuts and protein (beans, meat, eggs) in the diet. Fortification of food (i.e. enrichment through adding vitamins, minerals and trace elements) is not usually feasible or effective in rural areas, where people mainly consume local produce. One exception is salt fortified with iodine; another is fortification of packaged flour (from wheat, maize, sorghum, millet), where this is centrally milled and consumed widely in rural areas, as in many areas of southern Africa.

Income and nutrition are linked to each other, but not closely in the short term
Communities with higher incomes tend to have less malnutrition, but the link is not very close for individual households experiencing increase or decrease in their incomes. Nor is there much difference in the incidence of malnutrition between households with somewhat different income levels in the same community (Berg 1987:6). Other factors, particularly the level of education of the women of the household, play a much more immediate role in promoting good dietary practices. Therefore, increases in income may be necessary for ensuring household food security, but they may not be sufficient in themselves to bring about improved nutrition.

The nutritional benefits of increased income may also depend on which member of the family earns the extra income: women's income is often assumed to be of greater benefit to the children since women tend to spend less on liquor and tobacco. But the children's nutrition may also worsen if the mother finds employment and leaves them in the charge of an elder brother or sister who does not feed them properly, or the absence of the mother may reduce vegetable growing at home.

The occupational source of the household's income does not seem to affect child nutrition in any consistent way. It is sometimes feared that when non-staple cash crops take over on arable land formerly used for growing a variety of foods there is greater risk of malnutrition. One Kenyan study of the impact of cash cropping on nutrition showed that incomes of households in cash cropping areas were often higher, and there were no significant differences in nutrition between the cash cropping areas and others, except in the case of sugar growing areas, where children were more likely to be stunted. This was put down to the children eating sugar cane ('empty calories'), thereby getting sufficient for their immediate energy requirements, but not for growth (Government of Kenya 1979:II 3–8). However, a later Kenyan study, in South Nyanza, showed sugar-growing farming families to have gained improved nutrition as a result of earning high incomes by switching to sugar (Kennedy and Coghill 1988:1079). An important question is whether local growing and consuming of vegetables is increased or decreased as cash cropping increases.

The overall conclusion is that that there are no clear and immediate relations between increases in income and nutrition. It depends very much on family practices. Therefore while larger, sustained increases in income are associated with improved nutrition, smaller increases may not necessarily bring nutritional improvements. Nutrition education and a raised community consciousness for child health becomes important in these cases.

Nutrition programmes should be kept simple but may need to include health and income components, particularly in remote rural areas
Nutrition is so closely linked to community health, livelihood and child rearing practices that nutrition projects are always faced with the dilemma between concentrating their resources on direct alleviation (mainly through feeding programmes) or spreading them, to try to reduce the underlying local causes of malnutrition. Manageability counsels simplicity and few components, an approach recommended by the World Bank after finding that its early 1980s programmes in Colombia, Brazil and Indonesia had too many components to be manageable (Berg 1987). But where the underlying issues are multi-sectoral it may be essential to deal with them. Thus programmes range from the multi-sectoral (like the Joint WHO/Unicef Nutrition Support Programme in Iringa, Tanzania) which are directed to improving the health and work environment as well as the household nutritional environment, to those which focus only on feeding the undernourished, as in the World Bank's infant and child feeding programme in Tamil Nadu, India.

Considerations in deciding the extent of the programme include:

o the objectives to be achieved;
o the time perspective;
o resources available for the programme;
o the extent to which the nutritional problem is concentrated in the household or caused by the disease environment, income, food, water and fuel markets (see Figure 2.1 on the local food security system).

Community involvement is essential for success
Self-help, active community involvement in management and monitoring of nutrition programmes are essential, and not only where finance, skilled personnel and vehicles for the programme are in short supply. Planning effective local participation is a challenge: 'The planning of this important dimension must take account of the often severe constraints on what can be done at local levels, the financial limitations of local organizations, the length of time required to bring even small actions to fruition, the tenacity

that must be exercised, and the variety of economic and other forces that lie beyond the control of the local groups' (Berg 1987:40). Household and community involvement in the WHO/Unicef Iringa nutrition programme was achieved through a structure of committees starting at the village level using a 'Three As' framework (Analysis, Assessment, Action), involvement of the ruling political party, and promotion of family and community record keeping on children's nutritional progress.

A functioning primary health care (PHC) system is a major asset in nutrition programmes
Primary health care provides basic health care, mainly (but not only) to infants, small children and mothers. An adequate primary health care system, ideally organized through clinics, or if they cannot be afforded, through village level health care workers, is a major asset in combating malnutrition, since the people most vulnerable to malnutrition (mothers and infants) use the clinic or health worker most. The PHC system is a means for both measuring and for relieving nutrition problems by curing illness, and providing supplementary feeding and nutrition education. However, although commitment to universal primary health care is a basic tenet of health care policy in most countries (following the Alma Ata declaration of 1978) few countries in fact manage to provide it on a comprehensive scale. Therefore rural nutrition programmes must usually cope without a well-developed PHC system. Working closely with the existing local health care system, however rudimentary, is essential and instrumental in the improvement of both PHC and nutrition.

Finding out whether there is a nutrition problem in the area

This section supplements Chapter 2 by providing some guidelines on establishing and measuring the extent of malnutrition locally.

Four measures are commonly used. These are called anthropometric measures because they involve the measuring and weighing of people.

Weight at birth
Low birthweight (less than 2.5kg) is closely associated with nutritional problems in the mother during later pregnancy, and indicates likely nutritional problems to follow for the child. Comprehensive information on birthweights is unlikely to be available, since in rural areas with dispersed populations it is not common for births to take place at hospital or clinic, nor under supervision of a trained midwife, so birthweight is not usually measured. Improved training for traditional birth attendants (TBAs) and providing simple weighing scales and record cards can fill this gap. In the meantime, taking a small sample (approximately 30) of the weights of babies born in the locality may be informative.

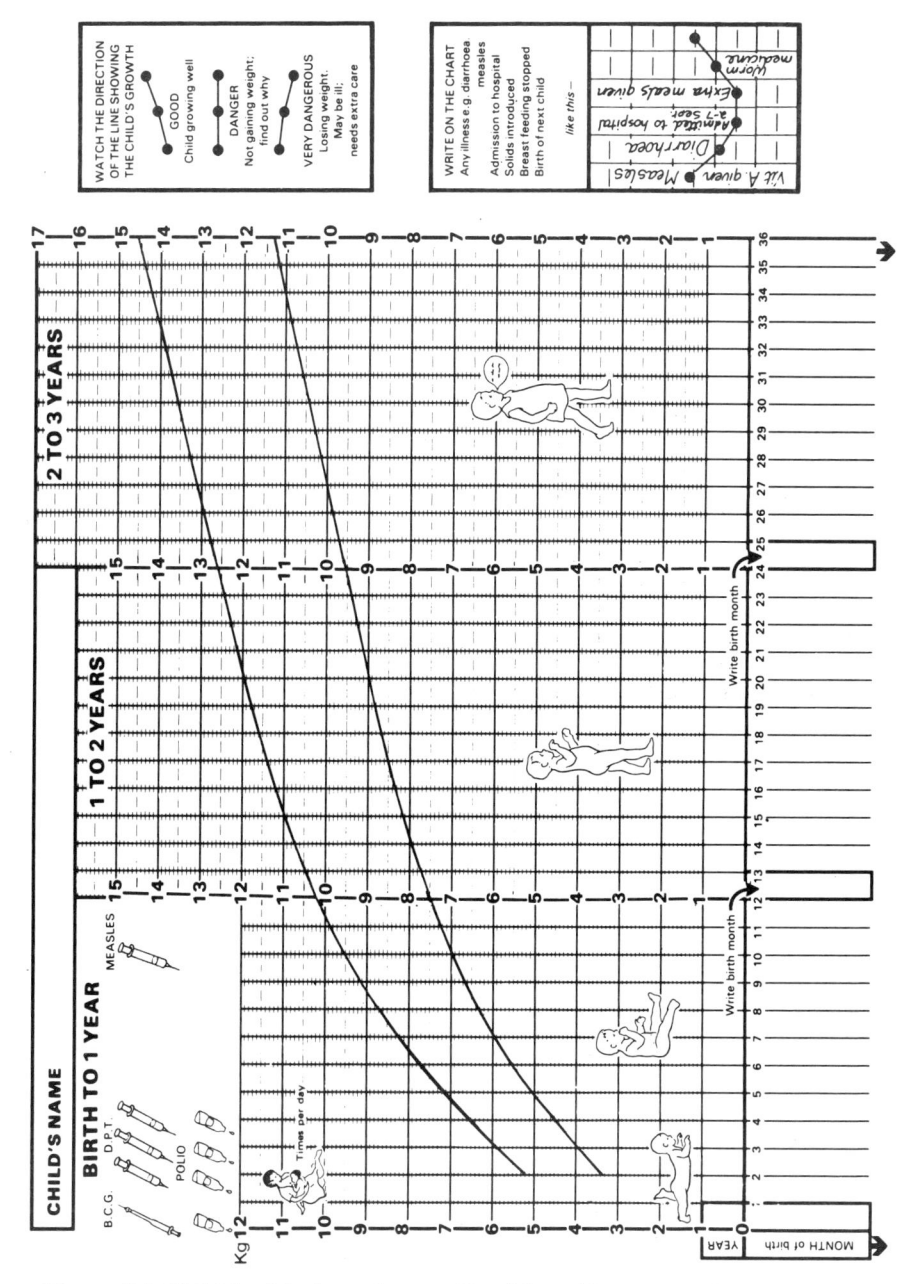

Figure 3.1 *Child health chart. Source:* Teaching-aids At Low Cost

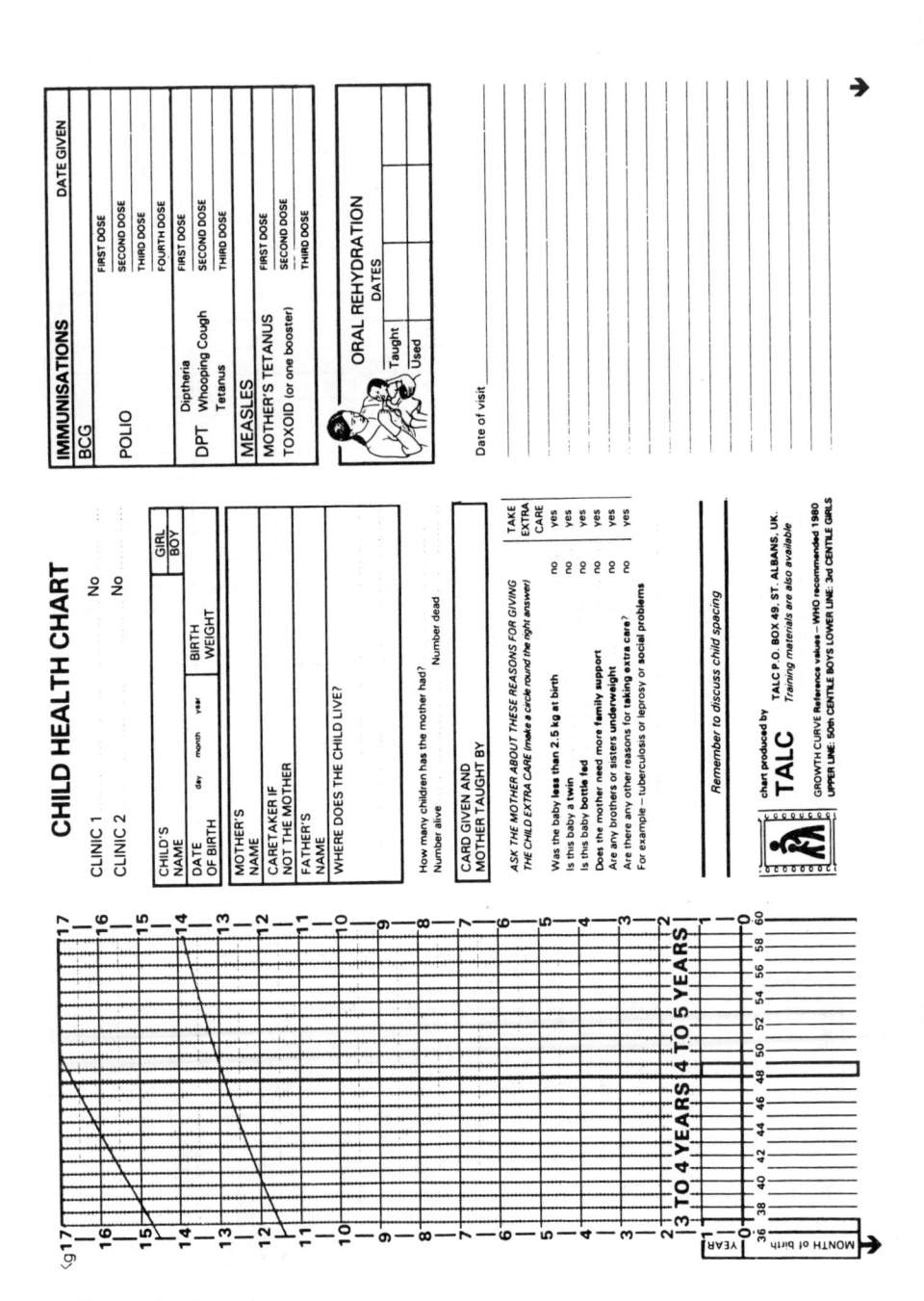

Figure 3.1 (cont.)

Weight for age
This is the weight of the young child (usually between one and five years) as a percentage of the normal weight for that age, where normal is the average by national or international standards. Below 80 per cent of normal weight strongly suggests inadequate nutrition. Measures of normal levels of weight and height in relation to age may be available for your country or region. Figure 3.1 shows a typical Weight for age chart, with its band of normal values within which the child's weight should lie.

Height for age
As for weight for age, but using height instead. Below 90 per cent of normal height for age is often taken to indicate stunting.

Weight for height
This is used together with the height for age measure. If the child's ratio of weight : height is below 80 per cent of the normal level, wasting due to undernourishment is probably the cause.

Other measures, such as infant mortality (deaths per thousand births during the first year of life), and morbidity (number of people contracting a disease per thousand of the population), are often used at national level. But, at local rural level, the information is unlikely to be available, since such information is not usually gathered and kept locally, unless there is a hospital in the area with good records.

How to collect the information
Three methods are common (Casley and Kumar 1987):

1. Attach a nutritional section to a household survey that is taking place anyway. This may involve little extra cost beyond training the enumerators to administer the anthropometric tests, and it may enable nutritional status to be judged by such variables as: area, household size, type of crops grown, occupation of household head, or whether the mother has a job. Nutrition in poorer rural areas usually varies with the time of year, the pre-harvest period often being the one when food is scarcest. It is important, therefore, that the survey takes this into account, preferably by collecting data from the same sample of people at different times of the year.

    In the case of household surveys being carried out to plan or evaluate a rural development project, it may be desirable to attach a nutritional section to the survey – especially in the case of projects which involve considerable changes in the way that poorer people earn their living, such as switches from food to cash crops, or resettlement programmes.
2. Community weighing programmes can be carried out at given intervals in selected areas, in which a sample of local children (or all) are

Box 3.1 *Severe malnutrition reduced by 70 per cent in four years, at $16.95 per child per year*

The Iringa Nutrition Support Programme is one of 18 initiated by WHO and Unicef in 1980 under Joint WHO/Unicef Nutrition Support Programme (JNSP). Iringa is a large, predominantly agricultural area stretching from the centre of Tanzania to the south-west border.

It was selected because of its high rates of malnutrition, diverse agro-ecological zones and its relatively strong institutional structure and also to build on existing Unicef co-operation with Iringa in water programmes.

The programme began in 1984 on a pilot basis covering 46 000 under-fives in 168 villages of 28 wards in six districts, and was expanded in 1987 to cover all the region's 600 villages, with a total under-five population of 239 000.

Components

- *Programme policy and communication:* Quarterly newsletter; information exchange; support to youth and cultural groups; production and showing of films on the programme.
- *Monitoring and evaluation:* community-based growth monitoring organized by village health committees, supported by village health workers: all under fives registered and provided with growth cards and weighed at village health posts every three months; counselling to parents of underweight children; records of child deaths and causes.
- *Integrated training:* Formation of training co-ordinating committee which conducted training with district multi-sectoral teams, who in turn trained at the ward level; training manuals developed and produced; multi-purpose training centres constructed.
- *Mother and child health:* Construction, renovation and equipping of dispensaries; training and equipping of village health workers, dispensary staff, traditional birth attendants and traditional healers reduced walking distance to the nearest health facility to no more than 5km. Sustainability through remuneration of village health workers by village governments in about 80 per cent of villages.
- *Water and environmental sanitation:* Villager-to-villager training in latrine construction, but demand for their skills generally poor partly owing to high cost of cement; water programmes pre-existing.
- *Household food security:* Analysis at village level of reasons for household food insecurity; promotion of simple models of household food requirements; development of weaning food manual and improved weaning food, including germinated cereal (*kimea* or 'power flour', as it is known locally, because of the high nutrition value) which reduces dietary bulk and viscosity, enabling children to consume more energy; promotion of drought-resistant crops in drought prone areas by supplying improved seeds and seed multiplication farms; rearing of small animals to provide animal protein, home gardens, simple techniques of food preservation, support to marginal farmers; improved seeds and seed multiplication farms; rearing of small animals to provide animal protein, home gardens, simple techniques of food preservation, support to marginal households by supplying them with farm inputs, training of agricultural extension staff on problem identification in household food accessibility, provision of 60 handmills to day-care posts in villages without grain mills, diesel driven mills provided to villages through credit scheme. A summary of food security problems, causes and interventions is in Table 3.1.

Table 3.1 Selected food security interventions in Iringa Nutrition Programme

Problem	Possible causes	Programme intervention
1. Inadequate food in households (most severe a few months before harvest)	☐ Lack of household planning ☐ Choice of wrong crops ☐ Failure of rains ☐ Poor crop management ☐ Storage losses ☐ Shortage of inputs ☐ Lack of income to buy food	☐ Training of trainers on household food planning ☐ Promotion of drought-resistant crops such as sorghum, sunflower, cowpea and especially cassava ☐ Improved storage
2. Inadequate nutrient intake (especially in children)	☐ Poor economic resources ☐ Nutritionally poor diet ☐ Shortage of fuelwood ☐ Shortage of fruits and vegetables ☐ Scarcity of meat ☐ Scarcity of beans and other legumes ☐ Too much workload for mother	☐ Promotion of income-generating activities ☐ Nutrition education especially to mothers through health workers ☐ Training and inputs for village afforestation and home gardening ☐ Training and inputs for small animal keeping ☐ Promotion of grain milling and appropriate technology
3. Lack of awareness of good weaning practices	☐ Lack of awareness of children's nutrient needs ☐ Inadequate feeding frequency ☐ Scarcity of energy-dense foods such as groundnuts and cooking oil ☐ Dietary bulk	☐ Provide weaning recipes based on local foods ☐ Mobilize communities to provide extra food at child care post ☐ Campaign on use of *kimea* ('power flour')

Source: Unicef (1989) p.12

○ *Child care and development:* The main problem is the extremely tight daily time schedule mothers must keep and the lack of effective child caretaker organizations, which result in infrequent child feeding. A total of 429 village day-care posts were established in all programme villages, providing child care and feeding using village resources, with attendants paid by communities. There was also provision of cooking utensils to centres, training of 683 day-care attendants, establishment of 31 pre-schools, training of 61 pre-school teachers, and training of village leaders in child care awareness. Interventions to reduce women's workload included: over 13000 improved stoves constructed by village artisans trained in the programme, in use in nearly 50 per cent of homes; training of craftsmen to make handcarts and wheelbarrows using simple tools for transport of firewood etc.; and agroforestry for households and villages, emphasizing firewood species.

o *Income generating activities:* Support through a revolving fund to six women's groups producing sunflower oil. All generated financial surpluses by 1990.

Features of the programme

o Programme management integrated into existing administrative and CCM party structure at regional, district, ward and village levels, through mass mobilization of leaders.
o Priority to those parts of the programme most wanted by the communities, i.e. mother and child health care, child growth monitoring, followed by the more complex interventions such as family planning.
o Village-based nutritional status and monitoring system stimulates participation of parents and community in child growth and development activities.
o 'Analysis, Assessment, Action' approach used at every level for continuous monitoring and improvement.
o Supplementary feeding of infants and young children using village resources without donated food.

---

measured, as in the Iringa programme (see Box 3.1). Indonesia and the Philippines have community weighing programmes in which the heights and weights of children are recorded twice yearly in selected areas (Casley and Kumar 1987:147). The growth chart record cards which are the basis for the community weighing programmes are usually kept by the mother, so she can monitor the child's growth, but the data should also be recorded and analysed so that the overall changes in nutritional status in the locality can be measured and reported back to the community.

3. Schools and clinics can be the location for nutritional surveillance and action. Clinics, if available, are the most suitable for infants and small children. School teachers can become important allies in nutritional surveillance of older children. Clinics and schools provide continuity in that anthropometric measurements can be made and reported routinely – this is most important if changes in nutrition over time are to be assessed. The information collected from schools and clinics will, of course, not necessarily be representative of the population of the area as a whole, if not all children go to schools, or not all infants attend clinics. It is often remarked that poverty is most likely to be hidden from the main streets, in rural as well as in urban areas, in that the poorest people

> *Successes of the programme*
>
> - Reduction in rates of severe and moderate malnutrition by 70 per cent and 32 per cent respectively between 1984 and 1988.
> - Deaths from diarrhoea and measles reduced.
> - Establishment of a community-based child care system and rehabilitation system for severely malnourished children.
> - Establishment of a village-based system to monitor child nutritional status and deaths.
> - Full immunization coverage increased from 56 per cent to 92 per cent.
> - National decision to adopt the Iringa approach in other regions.
>
> *Continuing challenges*
>
> - Seasonality in trends of malnutrition and child deaths which appear to be higher in the January–May period, which is the rainy season when risk of infectious diseases increases and mothers work long hours in agriculture and have less time for child care.
> - Diarrhoea and malaria are still the main child killers, particularly in rainy season.
> - Generating further local resources to improve child survival and assist marginal households.
> - For local councils to fill the gap in local services left by reduced government expenditure resulting from structural adjustment.
>
> *Sources:* Unicef (1989)
> Unicef (1990)

are the ones most isolated from education and health facilities. Where this is the case, information collected from schools and clinics needs to be supplemented by community weighing programmes.

In addition to these three formal methods of collecting nutritional information is the training of health workers to recognize visually when a child is malnourished, thereby enabling them to perform a 'health scout' role useful both for rapid appraisal of child nutrition in a neighbourhood and for monitoring. This approach has been used in health programmes in Zimbabwe.

Finally, a note of caution concerning information collection: investigation of the extent of malnutrition combined with little or no effort to relieve it is a recipe for resentment, suspicion and future non-cooperation among local people. Particularly at times of greater nutritional stress, such as during droughts or in the aftermath of floods, relief must obviously take precedence over evaluation. Ideally, evaluation and relief should be combined.

Designing programmes to improve nutrition

The components and priorities of nutrition programmes differ according to local needs. Involvement of community representatives and local women's organizations in identifying local nutritional problems and designing the programme is fundamental. Urban programmes tend to emphasize access to food (e.g. food stamps and rations) and may or may not include the components usually found in rural programmes. Programmes in rural areas usually include some or all of the following.

Core components (i.e. directly involving mother and child)

o supplementary feeding (food and micronutrients) to infants and mothers
o nutrition education to mothers
o raising of nutrition awareness in the community.

Preventive components

o sanitation: latrine construction, public awareness campaigns
o water source improvement: cleaner, cheaper, more plentiful water
o income generation: microprojects (tools and training) for the poorest, e.g. clothes making, repairs
o food production: demonstration plots, school gardens, seeds and tools.

Some key points to note in designing programmes

Understand the root cause of the problem
The purpose of including the preventive components is to reduce the root causes of the nutrition problem. But caution is needed since the root causes may not be obvious. For example, home, village and school gardening projects depend only partly on tools, seeds, water, fertilizer and pest control; the critical input in short supply may be labour time. Similarly, improved water and sanitation does not mean that people's health will automatically improve, since the way people use the cleaner water supply, how they store the water at home, and their washing habits, all determine whether the water consumed will still carry communicable diseases. In the case of latrines and drains, it is also a question of people's habits: provision of a latrine does not mean that it will be used and properly maintained. One sanitation project in India found that people were not using the new latrines because they preferred defecating in the open, regarding the latrines as smelly and frightening because of the deep pit.

Administrative arrangements must be locally appropriate
Administrative tasks multiply with the number of components in a programme, requiring increased division of labour and more active coordination. A basic decision is whether to set up a separate administrative unit locally to manage implementation or to fit programme activities into the duties of existing departments of local government. A compromise arrangement is often possible and desirable, whereby the programme office and staff are located within a department. Some departmental staff may be assigned to the programme, thereby maximizing communication

between programme and department while improving the department's capacity. There are no standard answers, it depends on local needs and circumstances.

The nutrition programme and the local health care system must work together

There obviously needs to be a close link between the core components of the programme (mother and child activities) and the local clinics, health workers and primary health care system. Where that system is in place and in good order, as in the case of Botswana's network of well-supplied rural and urban clinics, it provides the infrastructure for the core activities of nutrition programmes. In other cases, such as the NIPP programme in Indonesia, the nutrition programme provides the basis on which to establish a network of mother and child medical care. Where the health care system is poorly developed or badly run down and resources for building it up are scarce, the nutrition programme may be obliged to take on more responsibilities, as in the WHO/Unicef nutrition programme in Iringa (see Box 3.1).

Nutrition programmes should start small and on a pilot basis

Although most of the best known programmes are large, they generally started with small, pilot projects requiring few resources. This is particularly important in the case of rural projects which depend much more on local foods, food habits and organizations.

Supplementary feeding issues

Who?

Principally mothers and young children up to three years are the most in need.

How?

Clinics and creches, as part of the mother and child health programme. Where there is no functioning system of clinics and health posts, then through village health workers, or nutrition scouts, or village child nutrition committees.

What?

Local weaning food. It is important that local foods be used to ensure availability and familiarity with preparation.

What about other people besides mothers and infants?

Except in near famine conditions, supplementary feeding for older children and adults other than pregnant or nursing mothers normally takes low priority. School feeding schemes (not school gardens projects) tend to be expensive, become heavily reliant on aid, do not necessarily lead to improved nutrition, and are difficult to phase out. Nutrition of girls aged 8–12 is important, in order to avoid future obstetric problems caused by stunting; but this is probably best identified and dealt with through village health workers, or nutrition scouts visiting the family, and through nutrition education. School vegetable gardens and nutrition education as part of the curriculum are the most important nutrition interventions in schools.

What about severely undernourished children?
Severely undernourished children need intensive supplementation, either at home under the guidance of a health worker, or at a nutrition rehabilitation centre, or hospital. A severely malnourished child has greatly reduced resistance to disease. Oral rehydration salts (ORS), distributed prepackaged ready for dilution in clean water, or as a home-made dilute mixture of sugar, salt and clean water (eight teaspoons of sugar, one of salt in three ordinary-sized soft drink bottles of clean water), has been widely promoted in recent years as a cheap and effective means to prevent infant deaths from diarrhoea and vomiting.

What are the main problems with supplementary feeding programmes?
Supplementary feeding programmes can easily be seen as free handouts, which may then lead to corruption and dependence. The way to avoid this is to link them to family and community participation in a spirit of treating malnutrition as a disease, so that the supplementation becomes a medicine to deal with it, and mothers (preferably groups of mothers, as in the Tamil Nadu and Iringa programmes) become involved in recognizing the signs of malnutrition, understanding weight and height for age charts, and seeing the progress that their children make as their growth rate recovers.

Staffing can be a severe problem for supplementary feeding programmes, through unavailability of funds for qualified nutrition staff, or when qualified staff are unwilling to work in remote areas, or insist that underlings do the real work, or become frustrated with their career advancement being too slow. At the other extreme is the appointment of village health workers at very low levels of pay and status, with excessive expectations of what they can achieve. Village health workers, working together with women's groups, do provide the most cost-effective means to improve nutrition in mothers and children. But their tasks must be limited and specified, and their effectiveness will depend on the mothers' involvement and co-operation and the back-up they receive from government or the NGO responsible for the programme.

Nutrition education issues
Many mistakes have been made in nutrition education, as in agricultural extension, mainly because of an inadequate 'message' in the hands of the nutrition educator, and because of education being seen as a one-way system.

What does not work in nutrition education?
In rural areas, particularly where food habits and foods vary between localities, standard textbook recommendations to 'feed your child more green vegetables' may be ineffective and give nutrition education a bad name in the community. It can even result in worsening of nutrition in families who adopt the message, as happened in northern Nigeria (see Box 3.2) where recommendations of earlier weaning, and against the local weaning food, were found to have worsened malnutrition.

What is the basis of successful nutrition education in rural areas?
Outside of schools, where helping to run a school vegetable garden and learning the nutritional value of what is produced is the most valuable nutrition education, successful nutrition education involves working with mothers either as part of a supplementary feeding scheme, or in assisting

---

Box 3.2 *Correcting a nutrition education programme*

In northern Nigeria, in the late 1960s, the nutrition message being promoted by nutrition educators was to wean children at three months with a soft 'pap', made with water and cereal flour combined with a mashed protein-rich food, such as an egg, while young children should receive plenty of vegetables, fruits and juices. When the programme was evaluated the nutritional status measurements suggested that nutrition education was having a negative impact: earlier weaning often reduced rather than improved the babies' condition; the weaning 'pap' recommended was inferior to the local *saab* weaning food, normally administered between 7 and 12 months, and required more water, which was often contaminated.

The problems facing mothers were:

- being unable to afford the recommended foods ('These nurses tell us to give our children more groundnuts and beans, when we can't even give them millet');
- long working hours;
- laborious and slow cooking methods, partly as a result of fuel costs causing small children often to miss the evening meal because they were asleep before it was ready.

The recommendations for change included more participative nutrition education in the villages (not only in the health centres); food supplements at 5–6 months with a cheaper local 'multi-mix'; and a health, agriculture and nutrition (HAN) programme, supported by the relevant ministries, to deal with pressing problems of income, water and fuel, which stand in the way of better nutrition.

'Many nutrition educators "blame the victim", and aim to change the practices of individual mothers. Advice does not deal with real problems, or match the resources and opportunities of the mother. This type of education increases guilt and anxiety, but does not enable parents to change their situation.'

Source: Gordon (1984)

them to make more effective use of available foods, which is better done in groups to enable sharing of knowledge.

What skills does the nutrition educator need?
Sound technical knowledge of food requirements is needed, and social skills in bringing people together to discover their particular problems and share suggestions. Also required are flexibility, patience and an interest in finding local solutions to local problems combined with an appreciation that there may be no ready-made technical solutions to many family problems that affect nutrition (such as mothers in employment unable to find the time to prepare nutritious food, and to make sure that the children get it; or for those without employment, unable to find the money to buy nutritious food).

A key issue for nutrition educators is likely to be finding ways of preparing nutritious food quickly, perhaps in the form of a snack food (which reduces the likelihood of it being treated as a substitute for meals), which retains its quality, and is based on locally available ingredients. If the problems of working mothers are found to be important in malnutrition, nutrition educators also need to be able to deal with employers, in order to promote creche facilities and to encourage them to give mothers time to breastfeed.

Summary

This chapter has provided more detail on the link between household food security, nutrition and disease outlined in Chapter 2 (see Figure 2.1 especially). It has stressed that:

1. There is growing confidence that high levels of under-five mortality and malnutrition can be greatly reduced at low expense, as communities adopt a child survival orientation. The WHO/Unicef approach stresses prolonged breast-feeding, use of Oral Rehydration Salts (ORS), child immunization against the six killer infections, growth monitoring of children, access to clean water and improved sanitation and cleanliness in food preparation and handling.
2. Increased household food security is frequently necessary to improve child health in rural areas but is usually not sufficient by itself.
3. Community involvement is the basis of nutrition improvement programmes.
4. Investigation of the extent of malnutrition is best carried out on a regular basis through the local health-system and with families and community groups monitoring children's growth.
5. In order to avoid the pitfalls in supplementary feeding and nutrition education, malnutrition needs to be regarded as a disease with supplementary feeding a medicine, while nutrition education should be built upon community assessment of local nutrition problems and improvement possibilities; it should not consist of a standardized 'message'.

CHAPTER 4
Food Supplies and Prices

As a rural manager at a time of rapid liberalization of rural food markets you might feel confused and uncertain about what the role of NGOs or government in food markets should now be. Perhaps you would welcome liberalization, particularly if you were working in a district in which food markets were officially controlled by government but in reality were dominated by parallel markets. Or you may be against it, fearing that the relaxing of price and movement controls will cause shortages, price instability and exploitation of consumers and farmers by traders.

The purpose of this chapter is to help you in your effort to understand how well local food markets work and what might be done to make them work better.

State and market

The roles of the state and the private sector should be and can be complementary and mutually reinforcing in making food markets work better. This may seem a surprising assertion since they have been presented so often as being in opposition to each other. But they are only in opposition where the state, or some buyers or sellers, are trying to control the market for their own purpose – usually to extract more from it than they could without controls, i.e. to make monopoly profits from it, in the case of buyers and sellers, or, in the case of the state, to feed the cities more cheaply or raise foreign exchange.

A well-functioning market absorbs less of the net price of the product, i.e. marketing costs are low, so that both producers and consumers benefit. In general, for food markets to function well solid back-up from the state is required, particularly where there are uncertainties about food supplies, food quality or the stability of people's purchasing power.

State back-up
The back-up by the state has two parts:

1. Improving the market infrastructure and regulations
States have intervened in markets by regulation (improving regulations or removing them), participation (as buyer and seller), investment (investing

in the improvement of market facilities – whether these be market roads, shelters, stores, and whether the state is the sole investor or only provides the 'seed capital' to other private investors).

Some degree of market malfunctioning is present whenever there are poor conditions of competition, transport or communication among buyers and sellers. Improving rural food markets mainly involves the investment role of the state, plus ensuring that regulations help rather than hinder the good functioning of the market.

But since the investments which may possibly improve a market are almost limitless (roads, for example) and expensive in capital outlay and maintenance, it is important that the investments made are those which will actually improve the market. Further, in cases of poorly developed markets, investment in facilities may not be enough: entrepreneurs, with good market information and readily available working capital, may be too few to make the market work as well as it could. A frequent characteristic of poorly developed rural food markets is domination by one or two major traders carrying out the major transport, storage and processing, with numerous very small buyers and sellers assembling supplies from farmers or dispersing them to scattered consumers. The weakness in this structure may be a lack of medium sized traders offering competition to the large operators, often because they are restricted by regulations or licensing from doing so, or because they lack the capital, skills or encouragement. Skills training, improved market information and ability to compete for finance may help some smaller traders expand. These services to improved marketing are best provided by NGOs rather than directly by the state, but the state can encourage their provision. All the above factors indicate that the first step towards market improvement is to identify the main weaknesses in the market and the most appropriate investments to be made. Simple methods of investigation are discussed in the following section.

2. Preventing market failure

Market failure occurs where the market cannot function to meet the needs of buyers and sellers. 'Public goods' are defined by the inability of the market to distribute them effectively without public regulation and support. They include education and training for those unable to pay their cost, public health, environmental quality, infrastructure planning, justice and defence. In the case of food, there is market failure where a sudden reduction in food supplies or people's purchasing power occurs or threatens to occur. Where supplies of food have been disrupted, or there is fear they will be disrupted, as in a major drought, floods or war, food markets quickly fail: people hoard food, immediately buying any food that becomes available to create their own private stocks – thereby pushing up prices further. Less scrupulous suppliers may withhold stocks, confident of higher prices to come – raising prices still further. Under these circumstances, confidence in the market can only be restored by the state or community supplying food and thereby stabilizing prices. Where there is risk of food market failure the state must be able to increase supplies quickly in order restore people's confidence in the market.

The general conclusions regarding the state and the private sector in food markets are:

o They can be complementary, with the state providing the framework of minimum necessary regulations (to ensure quality and competition), and the private sector the capital, initiative and competitive drive.
o The more efficiently the market works and the less the risk of market failure, the less intervention is required from the state (i.e. the less the state needs to participate in the market as a buyer or seller).

Techniques for finding out how well local food markets work

A detailed understanding of how food markets work does require a lot of data that can only be acquired by thorough record keeping. But use of simple techniques of analysis and quick methods of collecting information can go a long way towards clarifying the overall workings of the food market, identifying the main problems, and the interventions that may be appropriate.

Seasonal calendars
The construction of seasonal calendars is outlined in Appendix I and illustrated in Figure 8.1 on page 111. Seasonal calendars, constructed by individuals or groups in each of the main farming systems in the district, can provide a variety of information, such as the seasonal variation in rainfall, tasks and products in agriculture and livestock production, labour migration, savings and debt, disease, changes in food stocks, extent of self-provisioning, food purchases and sales, price variations and seasonal changes in diet and hardship. The seasonal calendar is thus a valuable tool for local people to describe their situation and the main seasonal food problems in the area. It can also serve to indicate which food markets may be particularly inefficient (i.e. are indicated to be too high cost or too unstable) and for which the marketing chain should be examined more closely.

Marketing chain diagrams
A marketing chain shows the stages through which the commodity marketed passes from the producer, or from its point of entry into the area, to the consumer (see Box 4.1). Its usefulness is that it provides the basis for more detailed analysis, and that it can show roughly but at a glance:

Box 4.1 *Ruha parish: marketing chains for maize*

A fictional case study is outlined below to demonstrate the usefulness of a marketing chain investigation.

Ruha parish has three villages and a population of about 2000, living mainly on scattered farms. It is about 50 miles from the nearest town. The staple crop is maize, grown under rainfed conditions. The Ruha valley is quite fertile but subject to occasional drought. It usually exports maize in the half year after the harvest, but also imports maize meal for village dwellers and farming households who do not produce or store sufficient for their own yearly requirements. It is quite inaccessible, since the main road to the town negotiates a mountain pass and is in poor condition. There are two or three small retailers in each of Ruha parish's villages. In the larger village there is also a co-operative society shop with a warehouse for storing maize which is usually sold outside the parish. The retailers and co-operative shop also sell

Ruha parish: marketing chains for maize post-harvest half year, 1993

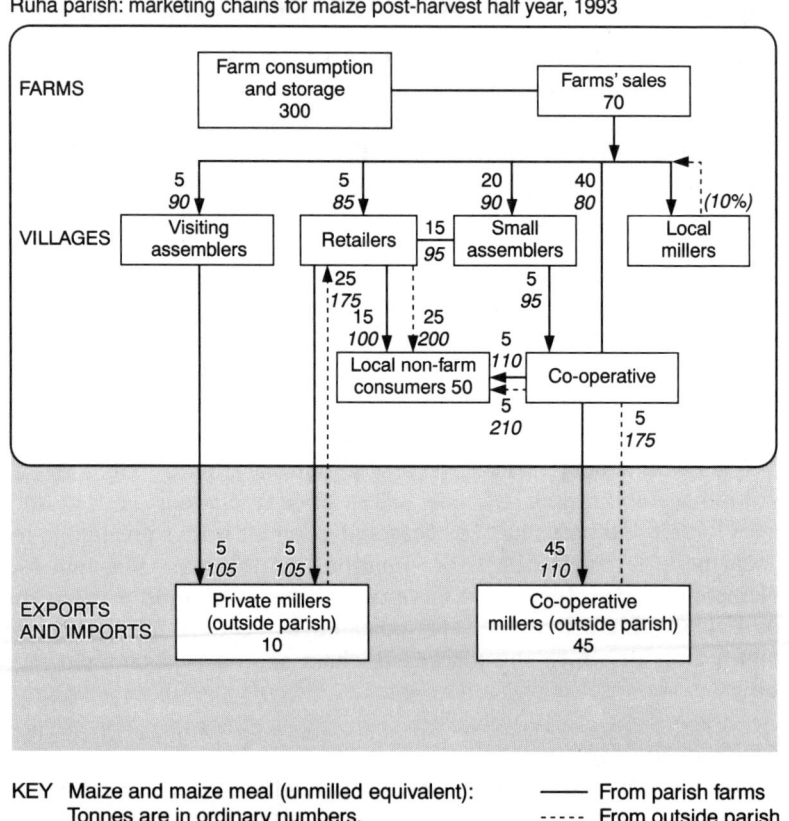

FARMS

Farm consumption and storage
300

Farms' sales
70

VILLAGES

5 90 Visiting assemblers
5 85 Retailers 15 95
20 90 Small assemblers
40 80 Local millers (10%)

25
175
15   25
100 200

5 95

Local non-farm consumers 50

110
Co-operative

5

5
210

5
175

EXPORTS AND IMPORTS

5 105
5 105

Private millers (outside parish)
10

45 110

Co-operative millers (outside parish)
45

KEY Maize and maize meal (unmilled equivalent):
Tonnes are in ordinary numbers.
Prices ($ per tonne) are in *italics*

——— From parish farms
----- From outside parish

☐ Parish boundary

maize meal in packaged form, bought in from private millers and the co-operative miller in the town. The Ruha co-operative is the main export channel in the post-harvest period. Until recently there was no local milling of maize other than grinding and stamping in the home. Two diesel hammer mills have recently been set up by individuals and are doing brisk business milling maize for households. They charge 10 per cent of the value of the maize for the service.

Local people complain of the high price of maize meal, especially in the pre-harvest season when supplies bought in from outside the parish provide much of the local requirements. Farmers complain of low prices they receive for maize, particularly from the co-operative which is the largest single purchaser. Some politicians point to the post-harvest sales from the parish and pre-harvest buying in, saying this must mean that local storage capacity is inadequate. The local council has taken up the complaints and asked the administration to investigate and report. After preparing seasonal calendars with local farmer and village groups and gathering estimates of average purchases, sales and prices from retailers and the co-operative, marketing chains for maize are constructed, as shown in the diagrams.

The following observations can be made from the marketing chains:

1. The marked difference between the pre-harvest and post-harvest period. In the pre-harvest period the trade is exclusively in packaged maize meal

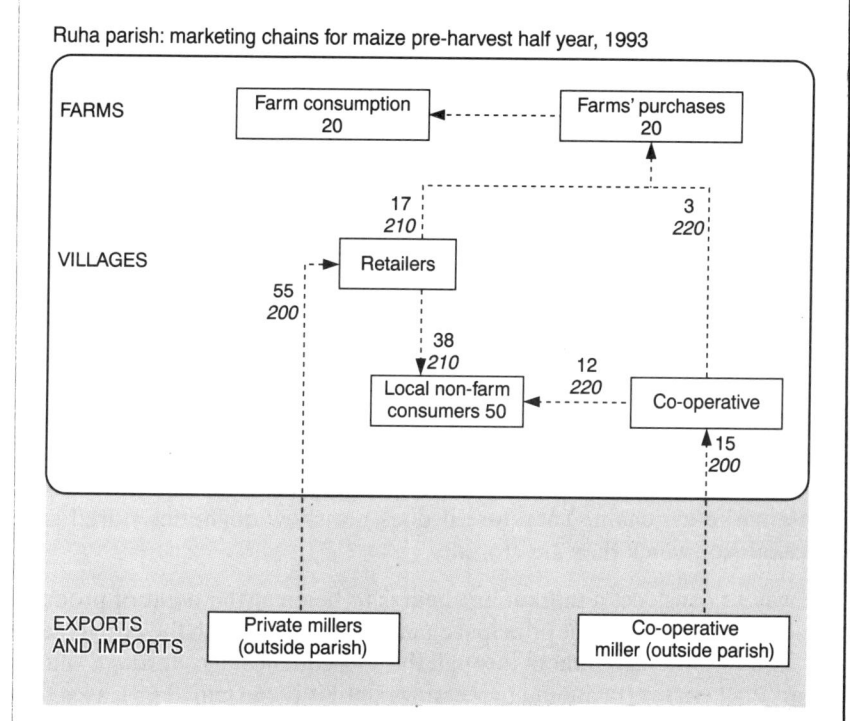

Ruha parish: marketing chains for maize pre-harvest half year, 1993

```
FARMS          Farm consumption  ←------  Farms' purchases
                      20                         20
                                                  ↑
                       17 :                    3 :
                       210:                    220:
VILLAGES           Retailers
               55 :
               200:
                         38
                        ▼210           12
                   Local non-farm     220
                   consumers 50  ------  Co-operative
                                             ▲15
                                             :200

EXPORTS        Private millers         Co-operative
AND IMPORTS    (outside parish)        miller (outside parish)
```

> bought in; in the post-harvest season, assemblers of maize operate, gathering loads which they sell to the co-operative and the retailers, who in turn supply local non-farm consumers and sell to the millers outside the parish.
> 2. The bulk of local production (300 out of 370 tonnes) is stored and consumed on farms; 55 of the 70 tonnes sold by farms is sold outside the parish, mainly to the co-operative miller in the town, even though the co-operative pays lower prices.
> 3. Local non-farm consumers are supplied mainly through the small retailers (who sell more cheaply than the co-operative) and they consume mainly packaged maize meal (35 out of the 50 tonnes of unmilled maize equivalent in the post-harvest period, and all of the 50 tonnes consumed in the pre-harvest period).
> 4. The cheapest source of maize meal is the two small local millers who charge only 10 per cent of the value of the unmilled maize for their service, while packaged maize meal at the retailers and co-operative is about twice the price of unmilled maize. It was not possible to estimate the quantities that they mill.
> 5. Additional off-farm storage of unmilled maize is probably not a need, since the seasonal price difference (10–15%) is probably lower than interseasonal storage costs. An estimate of storage costs is made in order to check this (see Box 4.2). The quality of on-farm storage is a

- quantities distributed through different channels;
- prices at which the commodity changes hands at each stage;
- shares of the final retail price paid to producers, wholesalers, processors and retailers, and the gross margins they receive;
- how different marketing chains compare in terms of the prices received by producers and consumers.

Its limitations are:

- It is static, i.e. it shows the picture only at a point in time. This picture might well represent the situation in a particular season but will not apply for the whole year. Particularly in the case of food markets, a district may export food in the post-harvest period but import food by the middle of the dry season.
- It applies only to one commodity, or group of commodities, e.g. vegetables, food grains.
- It does not show how quickly the commodity or payments move along the marketing chain. Therefore it does not show quantities stored and periods for which they are stored.

The way to construct a marketing chain is to begin at the point of production, find out the different principal channels through which the crop is sold and then follow each of them through the subsequent stages through which the product passes (including processing) until it is consumed or leaves the area.

> problem. A ranking exercise on causes of crop losses (see Box 4.4) ranked on-farm storage losses through insects, rats and mould as the main cause of post-harvest losses.
> 6. The co-operative's gross margins on both purchases and sales of maize and maize meal are higher than the retailers' (40 per cent and 33 per cent higher in the case of whole maize and maize meal respectively), indicating that its unit costs are higher. But the majority of maize sales from the farms still goes to the co-operative because of its ability to buy, store and transport in bulk. A marketing costs analysis of the co-operative is recommended.
> 7. The main overall observation is that local milling of maize is low cost but the bulk of maize meal consumed is supplied by millers from outside the parish. This suggests that the local millers are unable to supply the local demand for packaged maize meal. Discussions with them while preparing the marketing chains indicated that they are fully occupied with service milling, would like to produce packaged meal in the future but fear that retailers and consumers would doubt the quality. The retailers confirmed that they would be cautious on quality grounds. The co-operative presently sells only its own brand. The Small Business Development department is urged to give attention to promoting local packaging of maize meal.

In the case of a marketing chain for food imports into the district, begin with the different channels through which food enters, tracing the stages through which it passes to the point of consumption.

The amount of information required for constructing marketing chains depends on the use to which the marketing chain will be put. An overall view of local marketing chains, and approximately how significant they are in terms of quantities marketed, may be all that is required at first. The information needed can be collected by interviews with producers, traders and processors at different stages of the chain, which will also provide a quick and valuable insight into the many issues, problems and disputes in food marketing in the area.[1] Box 4.1 shows the usefulness of marketing chain investigation.

Average selling prices at each stage of the marketing chain should be included. These enable the *gross margin* at each stage to be calculated:

Gross margin = Selling price per tonne – Buying price per tonne.

No calculations of marketing costs are required initially. These may be looked at later, for particularly problematic segments of a marketing chain, or to compare marketing chains (see below).

DOs and DON'Ts in constructing marketing chains

Do

○ Begin with a small, local area (otherwise the chains may quickly become overcomplex).

- Begin at the source of the food, i.e. the producer or entry point into the area.
- Include estimates of the quantities (or per cent of total consumption or production in the area) and selling price at each link of the chain.

Don't forget

- Marketing chains are different in different seasons. Districts that export food after the harvest may be importing by the pre-harvest period. Constructing marketing chains post- and pre-harvest will indicate the difference.

A sketch diagram of the marketing chain – even if it is not particularly detailed – provides a focus for discussions with farmers, traders, consumers and local politicians, turning unstructured conversations into exchanges over specific characteristics of the chain, prices obtained, quality of the product and reliability of the chain. The main problem areas in the chain should emerge – i.e. those links that are felt to be most inefficient, high cost or unreliable – and it is these which become the focus for more detailed consideration using marketing costs analysis.

Marketing costs analysis

Analysing marketing costs provides the evidence for judging how well marketing chains are functioning. It enables comparisons to be made between:

- costs of alternative marketing chains;
- transport costs between villages compared to the price differences between them (to see whether *spatial arbitrage*, i.e. moving food from one village to another, is profitable);
- storage costs compared to seasonal price differences (to see whether *temporal arbitrage*, i.e. storing food after harvest for sale in the dry season, is profitable).

It also enables rates of profit to be estimated to indicate how profitable a particular marketing activity is compared to average rates of profit locally, for which the rate of interest charged on loans provides a rough indication.

Comparing costs in alternative marketing chains

The reasons for comparing different marketing chains are various but often include:

- comparing 'official' with 'unofficial' channels, where there are regulations restricting marketing to a marketing board or co-operative;
- comparing chains which use different means of processing (e.g. different milling or baking techniques).

The gross margin figures in the marketing chains enable overall comparisons to be made between marketing chains. An estimate of the profit made at any point in a marketing chain can be made by calculating the *net margin* per tonne:

Net margin = Gross margin/tonne − Marketing and processing costs/ tonne

But a note of caution! If one marketing channel gives a higher gross margin, but it is unreliable, or takes longer, or there are delays in payment, then producers may not prefer it.

Costs for the operations carried out in wholesaling, processing and retailing are needed in order to calculate net margins. A simplified account is presented in Box 4.2, which illustrates well how a large gross margin is reduced when processing costs are taken into account.

Some of the cost items – such as taxes, commission to agents and rents – are easily established. Typical transport costs too may be easily found out by consulting transporters. More difficult may be actual processing and handling costs: for these, actual records of inputs used, and their costs, will be needed.

Since the gross margin analysis will have identified the main problem areas in the marketing chain, net margin analysis need only focus on these. It is particularly well-suited to this task, since the more detailed

---

Box 4.2 *Simplified annual operating statement* ($)

Receipts:
Direct sale of rice	13 760
Parboiling, milling and other services	17 600
Total	31 360

Expenditure:
Direct purchase of paddy (150 tonnes)	13 120

Processing costs:
Manager and skilled	7 680
Casual labour wages	2 780
Rent of premises	480
Fuel	1 090
Depreciation	800
Mechanical repairs	450
Total	13 280
Total expenditure	26 400

Gross margin on direct purchases of paddy and sales of rice
= (sales proceeds − purchase costs)/tonnes
= (31 360 − 13 120)/150 = 200.27 per tonne

Net margin on direct purchases of paddy and sales of rice
= (sales proceeds − purchase costs − processing costs)/150
= (31 360 − 13 120 − 13 280)/150 = 33.06 per tonne

Source: Adapted from a case study from Illushi, Nigeria, in Abbott (1987)

look at the costs of the firm or firms involved can itself produce valuable discussion on the problems of the marketing system and possibilities of improvement.

How to use net margins
There are two results that emerge from a net margin analysis comparing marketing chains, or parts of marketing chains (e.g. different wholesalers or processors).

Firstly, a comparison of the cost levels per tonne can be made, seeing how different cost items compare, and thereby tracing the main reasons for the difference in gross margins and prices at that level in the marketing chains.

Secondly, the net margin is a measure of profit. It indicates how profitable the particular marketing activity is, by showing the surplus of revenues over costs, per tonne, as illustrated in Box 4.2.

Transport costs between villages compared to market price differences
A particularly useful technique for analysing the efficiency of a food marketing system is to compare price differences (per tonne) between market centres in the district, relative to the transport costs (per tonne) of moving food between them.

If the food market in the district is working well it will be reasonably well-integrated. This means that if, say, in April the difference between the wholesale price of grade 1 rice per tonne in A and B is substantially greater than the transport costs per tonne of moving that rice between A and B, traders will move rice between A and B until the price difference is reduced almost to the level of the transport costs between A and B. If the price difference persists at a level substantially above the transport costs then food marketing between A and B is inefficient.

Box 4.3 *Spatial arbitrage table*

How efficient is food marketing in the district? Price differences vs transport costs (per tonne)

Example: Rice, post-harvest season, where A, B and C are market centres in a district

From To		A	B	C
A	Price diff. Transport		100 80	120 115
B	Price diff. Transport	100 50		60 60
C	Price diff. Transport	120 110	60 50	

A simple way of testing this for a district is to construct a spatial arbitrage table as illustrated in Box 4.3. The main centres (villages or towns) of the district are arranged horizontally and vertically. The top number in each of the squares is the price difference per tonne and the bottom number the transport costs per tonne. Thus Column 'A' shows the price difference and transport costs between 'A' and each of 'B' and 'C'.

If the price difference number in any square exceeds the transport costs substantially (e.g. by 50 per cent) then the market does not work well between the two centres – as, for example, from A to B in the table, where the price difference is twice the level of transport costs.

Storage costs compared to seasonal price differences
If food prices in the district fluctuate greatly between seasons, the reason may be either:

○ failure of **spatial arbitrage**, if (as discussed above) price differences between markets are substantially greater than transport costs, in any or all seasons;

or

○ failure of **temporal arbitrage**, i.e. buying food after the harvest for storage and sale in the dry season.

Temporal arbitrage is inadequate if the difference between prices after the harvest and in the dry season is much greater than the costs of storing food for that period. The greater the uncertainty about storage costs and future prices, the less attractive temporal arbitrage becomes.

Costs of storage consist mainly of:

○ Costs of capital, i.e. the cost of borrowing, or using money for purchase and holding of food, including the rent on the storage facilities, and other incidental costs. This is measured by the rate of interest on the capital over the period.
○ Storage losses, i.e. deterioration and shrinkage of the stored food.

Getting accurate information on both of the above is difficult. But a quick estimate of whether storage costs are greater or less than seasonal price differences can be made by finding out:

○ *What monthly interest rates are charged on borrowing money locally?*
Local money lender rates, if these are the main option, can be used. They are often calculated in simple monthly rates, uncompounded, for periods less than a year. Thus 5 per cent interest per month equals 30 per cent over six months.
○ *What percentage of the crop stored is lost due to deterioration and shrinkage?*
Estimating storage losses requires some care since estimates vary greatly, even in the same district – partly because the term 'storage

Table 4.1 Seasonal price changes of maize

Example First grade, June 1990–March 1991 (Town A)

	1990 J	J	A	S	O	N	D	1991 J	F	M
Price (per tonne)	1000	1100	1100	1200	1200	1300	1400	1500	1800	1500
% of June 1990	100	110	110	120	120	130	140	150	180	150
% Change from June 1990	0	+10	+10	+20	+20	+30	+40	+50	+80	+50

losses' is often used to mean all post-harvest losses. A simple way of reducing this confusion is to construct a 'Causes of Crop Losses' table, as illustrated in Box 4.4 (page 59). But uncertainty will still remain and it is safer to settle on a range of likely storage loss percentages to use in this exercise.

o *What are the average seasonal price increases?*

This can be found out from traders by establishing what the average price by grade was in each month, then showing each monthly price as a percentage of the postage harvest price, as shown in Table 4.1.

A simple estimate of the cost of storage is made by subtracting the interest costs and the percentage of the value of the crop lost through deterioration during storage, from the value of the crop when put into storage. For example, if the monthly rate of interest is 3 per cent and the storage loss is 2 per cent per month, then the monthly storage cost is 5 per cent. This assumes that no additional transport, labour or materials costs are incurred in order to store the grain.

Temporal arbitrage is more likely to be inadequate than is spatial arbitrage since it is often more costly and almost always more risky, since future prices are uncertain.

Movement of food between places (spatial arbitrage) and storage (temporal arbitrage) both tend to make prices more stable over time and more similar among places, except in the rare cases where a monopolist controls supplies and can manipulate the market for profit. Better transport and communications, and greater numbers of suppliers make monopolistic control less likely.

What can be done to overcome problems

Having acquired an overview of the food markets of the district and the way they work; having learnt, from discussions with farmers, traders, processors and consumers, what the problems are; and perhaps also having analysed the marketing costs and prices at one or two points in problematic marketing chains; having done all this, the rural manager is faced with the task of what can be done, and what are the priorities.

Probably the most general food market problem found in remote areas is a 'thinness' of the market. This implies consumers and suppliers who are scattered, markets that operate only occasionally, with prices varying widely, and transport costs which are high. But this situation is mainly the result of a general lack of economic development in the area; any new development in employment creation or infrastructure can have a quite dramatic impact on food markets – on both the type of foods consumed and the integration of markets.

This does not mean that without increased economic development of a district the food markets cannot be improved. A key issue to examine is the impact of government activities. There may be changes that can be made in government participation, regulations or investment affecting food markets and supplies – some at specifically local level, others more wide ranging – which can improve food markets. Regulations may be inappropriate (e.g. on movement of food, or licensing, or prices). If government participates in local food markets (e.g. by distributing food aid, or by storing food) there may be ways of making this more effective. Or government investments may have been inappropriate (e.g. building unused market facilities) and require better planning in future.

Abbott and Makeham (1979: 59) identify some of the increased marketing costs which are caused by government, or can only be reduced by government:

> Municipal authorities may be dominated by local commercial interests and these often impede the adoption of efficient marketing procedures. Charges are made for which no service is received and this is frequently responsible for part of the gap between consumer and producer prices. Often, movement licences or permits and favourable transport or storage arrangements can only be obtained quickly by illicit payments in addition to the authorized charges. Even in the most 'advanced' countries there have been cases where goods have been damaged or delayed because they belonged to someone who attempted to dispense with the services of certain handlers and porters, or refused to pay for 'protection'. To escape from such exploitation it is essential that wholesalers feel able to develop outside channels and direct retailer supply links, and are afforded reasonable security in doing so. One step in improving urban food supply channels is to break group wholesaler monopolies sheltering under restrictive municipal regulations.

Some typical problems in rural areas, and suggested approaches to improvement, are discussed below.

Typical food distribution problems and suggested approaches to improvement

Distribution of food refers to the spatial movement of food – from the producer to the consumer. Typical distribution complaints include the following:

Transport costs are too high

A remote district necessarily has higher transport costs than an accessible one. Its roads are likely to be in much worse condition. But the inevitability of higher transport costs to an inaccessible area can easily lead to poor roads being blamed for more than they should be.

- *Lack of backloading* may put up transport costs. This occurs when food or other produce is transported into/out of the district but the trucks return without a payload.
- *Overpricing of transport.* Is excess profit being made in transport? Compare the costs of trucking per tonne per kilometre on different routes of similar road quality serviced by different truckers. How much competition is there among truckers? Interview the truckers to find out what problems they face which raise the costs.

Ultimately, investment in road improvement or maintenance is essential to reduce transport costs. But some existing interventions (e.g. taxing, licensing of vehicles) may raise costs.

Consumers and producers do not know whether prices in neighbouring areas are attractive or not

In remote areas, with poorly integrated markets, there may be a lack of up to date market information generally available to producers or consumers.

Dealing with this problem alone, i.e. without improvement of transport or communications, may not have much impact. But as part of an effort to improve markets, transport and communications, the following may be worthwhile:

- Local radio programmes or newspapers can be encouraged to broadcast and feature food price information.
- Local chambers of commerce may be encouraged to collect and publish price and market information.
- If price data are regularly collected and updated by government, e.g. as part of an early warning system, these can be posted up locally.

Red tape prevents the movement of food between districts

Many countries with large, low-income rural populations strictly regulate the movement of food between districts (e.g. India, Kenya). The intention is to prevent food shortages occurring in any district, and to maintain price stability and food security for the population. This is thought to be particularly important during droughts when food shortages occur in rural areas as food is moved to the cities or even exported, if these markets yield greater profits.[2]

The scandals of food exports from countries beset by famine (e.g. Ireland in the 1840s, Bengal in the 1940s, Sudan in the 1980s) is the major argument for controls, together with the desire to prevent profiteering on the internal trade by traders colluding with each other.

But undesirable as removal of food from a food shortage area during a famine is, restrictions on movement of food are not necessarily an effective way to keep rural food prices down.

This is particularly true if such restrictions are sweepingly and inflexibly applied, without measures to supplement local incomes (to boost local demand) and without delivery of food supplies sufficient to reduce consumers' and food traders' expectations that shortages will increase further in future. Expectations of shortage play a large role in actual food shortages, since they cause panic buying by consumers and retention of supplies by traders, in the expectation of further increases.

Problems with movement restrictions as the main policy instrument to prevent food price increases in deficit rural areas include:

1. The system of restrictions tends to be inflexible and may cause food prices to rise in deficit districts, thereby reducing food security.
2. Movement restrictions may cause food prices in a district to fluctuate more than they would with unrestricted trade, and to fluctuate less predictably thereby decreasing the incentive for temporal arbitrage. This occurred in western Sudan in the late 1980s, when restrictions on inter-district movements and erratic arrivals of food aid discouraged traders from inter-seasonal storage.
3. Restrictions on movement increase transport costs (by causing delays, or bribes to officials, or the use of illegal border crossings). The increases in prices caused by movement restrictions can be significant, as indicated in a recent study on cereals trade barriers in the Horn of Africa (IGADD 1990).

In summary, in normal times food movement restrictions are unnecessary and serve only to raise the price of food to the consumer and lower it to the producer. In times of impending shortage they are meant to keep food prices down and thereby protect the purchasing power of the poorest. But by themselves they are an inadequate and unreliable means of protecting purchasing power. Furthermore, direct means both of protecting the purchasing power of the vulnerable (e.g. employment creation, cash assistance) and of stabilizing prices (e.g. public sector stocks), work better if inter-district movement is allowed, since this makes food supplies more easily available. Cash assistance programmes in Ethiopia in the mid-1980s were adversely affected by lack of local food availability for purchase, owing to movement restrictions (Webb 1989).

Producers complain that there is no market for their perishable produce, such as vegetables and milk
The marketing chain investigation may have revealed, through discussions with farmers, that there are no market opportunities for perishable produce locally, beyond exchange with neighbours. This amounts to a break in the marketing chain.

The farmers may have complained that their supplies are not bought by local shops, which get their supplies from outside the district. The shopkeepers perhaps argue that local supplies are too seasonal and surpluses too uncertain for them to be relied upon.

This situation arises most often in food deficit areas where the main source of income is non-agricultural, e.g. a mining area, or where people are dependent on earnings from migrant labour, with food mainly being imported by shopkeepers and where there is little if any local market tradition.

While the obvious approach is to try to develop local open markets for produce, it must be remembered that simply providing market facilities does not create a market; if supplies are scanty and expensive the market may hardly be used. In general, produce markets emerge on the streets before provision of proper market facilities is necessary.

In this case the fundamental problem is one of production and quality of fruit, vegetables or milk, since the demand is there. Questions of raising production are discussed in the next chapter. If seasonal surplus and deficit are the problem then technical and financial assistance to farmers may be a way forward, combined with improved methods of storing for later consumption, such as cheese making, fruit and vegetable drying and preserving, which may also make the product more saleable.

Farmers complain of inadequate marketing board services
Marketing parastatals in most countries are now under great pressure to increase their efficiency and to fit in with an expanded role for private traders. They were set up widely in developing countries in the post-World War II years, with a variety of objectives:

- To control quality and quantity of product offered on home and/or domestic markets.
- To establish producer prices and, if necessary, to operate reserve stocks for this purpose.
- To control imports and exports of the product.
- To promote consumption of the product.

They operated mainly with the principal food grains (rice, maize, sorghum) – the so-called 'political foods' since, being the basic foods of most people, their prices are the most politically sensitive. Co-operative marketing societies have frequently been used as the assemblers of produce at local level, who then sell it on to the marketing board. With governments often keen to keep consumer prices down and producer prices up, marketing boards were often subsidized. By the 1980s, in Africa particularly, many marketing boards were in deep financial trouble, accused of inefficiency and corruption, offering lower prices to farmers than offered by private traders and supplying a smaller and smaller share of the urban markets, with debt-strapped governments less and less able or willing to subsidize them. In some countries they were abolished (e.g. Nigeria) and in others where they have survived they are under great pressure to increase their efficiency and fit in with an expanded role for private traders. The recent efforts to restructure the National Cereals and Produce Board (NCPB) in Kenya are a prime example.

Some marketing boards have a clearer record of success in achieving the objectives of stimulating production while stabilizing prices at an acceptable level; noteworthy are BULOG in Indonesia and the Food Corporation of India. But even in these cases large subsidies are required (see Abbott 1987).

Returning to the district, the local marketing board will probably therefore be either already in the process of reorganization or about to undergo it. It may therefore be a good time for farmers' complaints to be raised forcefully.

Frequent complaints include:

○ delays in payments
○ prices below commercial prices
○ restrictions on selling to private traders
○ too few collection and sales points.

Key issues to be focused on in discussion regarding the future role of the marketing board will probably be:

○ Should it compete with private traders?
○ Should it try to stabilize prices by inter-seasonal storage?
○ Should it provide emergency stocks during times of food shortages?
○ Is there room for improvement in the efficiency of its operations?
○ Is the private sector ready and able to step into the gap left by a reduction in the marketing board's activities?

While there is no way that national policy on food marketing is going to be set from the district level, there is every reason to try to influence policy as far as it applies to the district, since the role and effectiveness of a local marketing parastatal will be central to any strategy to improve food markets in the district.

Local marketing co-operatives are either inefficient and corrupt or dominated by large farmers and serving only their interests
Marketing co-operatives, owned by groups of farmers, play the major role in assembling grains, pulses and livestock products in most middle and high-income countries. They also often carry out the first stage of processing (e.g. pasteurization of milk or hulling of rice). The most successful co-operatives are run as businesses for the benefit of their members, who are usually established commercial farmers.

Farmers' and consumers' co-operatives were widely promoted by planners in the post-World War II period as a means of channelling inputs to farmers and marketing their produce, often to the similarly promoted marketing boards. Major managerial problems have occurred where co-operatives were promoted and put in place by governments and NGOs beyond the ability of the beneficiaries to run them properly. It is widely agreed now that building co-operatives 'from above' as an instrument of rural development policy is ineffective.

Co-operatives are essentially commercial organizations operating for the benefit of their members. As with any commercial company success is attained only if the co-operative attracts the energy, responsibility, commitment and involvement of its members. To achieve this, members must see a clear benefit for themselves from strengthening and sustaining the efficiency of the organization. Hence, co-operatives consisting of relatively few, relatively wealthy, educated members, each of whom participates in the decision-making of the co-operative, tend to succeed better than large associations of uneducated farmers with little capital and who are unable to control the appointed management. Large co-operatives of poor farmers can work (e.g. the Amal dairy co-operatives in India) but then they usually require charismatic leadership, plus a high degree of identity of the farmers with each other, and clear and immediate benefits to the individual member.

There is collusion among sellers (or buyers) of produce locally: they fix prices unfairly
The marketing chain and marketing costs analysis will have provided information on whether marketing costs in the district are excessively high or whether excess profits appear to be being made by marketing agents. If so, the first indication is that competition should be increased. This can be done by:

- licensing more traders to deal in basic foods, or removing licensing requirements altogether;
- relaxing movement controls to allow easier trade to and from the district;
- encouraging new traders to enter the business (assistance with training investment, trade credit);

- state or community participation in the market (through the local authority or a parastatal) by storing food and selling it at low prices to the poor, or selling when prices rise too high;
- improving roads, or vehicles, so that transport costs are lowered.

If price control on basic foods is supposed to be observed by traders locally but is in fact not, attempting simply to enforce it in the face of widespread disregard is unlikely to have much impact by itself – especially where high marketing costs are already squeezing margins. This is frequently the case in remote areas if government's food price controls have been based on urban cost levels. A combination of short-term sales by government or community, and longer term efforts to improve markets and local incomes, is called for.

The private traders are very weak – they have not responded to the opportunities offered by liberalization
Although regulations on licensing and movement controls have been relaxed, and the marketing board no longer dominates, private traders may not have responded well.

Commonly, remote areas have very few, often only one or two, relatively large traders and numerous very small traders – often buying from the large trader on a wholesale basis (in the case of food imported into the district) or selling to the large trader (in the case of grain or livestock purchases). There may be a lack of middle sized traders, growing from the ranks of very small traders, to provide real competition to the established large trader. In other words, the problem for small traders may not be one of *entering* the market but of *growing* as a business.

There are several reasons why new entrepreneurs either do not enter the market or remain very small, even where there are profits to be made from trading or storing food:

- *Lack of skills, confidence and capital.* Local culture may lack a strong trading tradition in families. This is recognizable by whether local traders are from the community or not. With economic development, trade becomes a more widespread source of employment for people, and it creates an environment encouraging families to engage in it. But potential entrepreneurs may require training in running a small business and assistance with obtaining capital.
- *Lack of market information.* But this problem may apply particularly to small traders and new entrants to trading.
- *Transport difficulties and costs.* Lack of vehicles, fuel or spares. Check efficiency of transport arrangements to and from the district (as discussed above).
- *Difficulties in obtaining supplies.* Particularly in remote food deficit areas, small traders can often only obtain supplies from a large trader,

who acts both as wholesaler (for very small sellers – who often buy only a few baskets-full to sell a few miles away) and as retailer in the main centre of the district. In this case the lack of competition is not in retailing so much as in the long haul to the district centre itself. Attracting competition into this wholesale sector may be difficult without expansion of the market. Find out from other wholesalers operating in other districts why they are not supplying this district and what would be necessary for them to do so.

Storage problems

Storage losses are too high
Estimates of storage losses vary greatly, even in the same district, often between 5–6 per cent and 20–30 per cent. A common reason is that storage losses are difficult to estimate: they include losses of quality as well as quantity; some of the loss may be partly recoverable (e.g. use of spoiled grain as animal feed); and the term 'storage losses' is frequently used loosely by farmers and grain handlers to cover post-harvest losses in general rather than storage losses alone.

If you wish to identify storage losses alone it is necessary to isolate them from other post-harvest losses and to take into account how storage losses may be increased by problems in crop drying, harvesting, shelling, threshing, winnowing and milling or stamping.

A quick, rough and ready way of separating out these different causes of losses for the locality is to make up a 'Causes of Crop Losses' table (see Box 4.4). The table should be filled in with the help of key informants, in this case knowledgeable farmers, grain traders, extension workers and researchers. The 'preference ranking' technique may be used, as described in Appendix I. The table avoids the thorny problem of measuring losses in terms of quantity or value by simply ranking causes of losses within the harvesting and post-harvesting stages of the crop, and then finally making an overall ranking among stages, to give an idea of where the greatest losses are occurring.

To fill in the table, ask the key informants or focus groups, to write rankings (1, 2, 3 etc.) against the causes in each stage in order to get an idea of their relative importance. Then finally write numbers next to each stage in order to get the informant's estimate of the stages at which the greatest losses occur. Do this separately with four or five key informants or groups independently, and compare the rankings that they make. If the rankings are on the whole similar you can be confident that the main causes of losses have been identified.

The most immediate benefit from a rapid investigation of this kind is to put storage losses in a wider context and to clarify the source of storage losses. This will help in avoiding inappropriate investments in storage

> **Box 4.4** *Rapid identification of causes of crop losses in harvesting and post-harvesting*
>
> Storage losses are often not distinguished from losses caused by poor harvesting. This exercise uses key informants (mainly grain farmers and merchants) to rank causes of crop losses.
>
> | **Problem** | **Rank** |
> |---|---|
> | *Harvesting:* | |
> | Late | |
> | Damp | |
> | Breakage | |
> | Soil contamination | |
> | *Post-harvest:* | |
> | Inadequate drying | |
> | Poor threshing | |
> | Poor winnowing | |
> | Rats and mice | |
> | Insect attack | |
> | Poorly designed store | |
> | Poorly maintained store | |
> | Inadequate fumigation | |
> | Inadequate turnover of grain | |
>
> *Method:* Discuss the causes of losses during harvest and post-harvest locally with key farmers, or focus groups of grain farmers and merchants. Ask them to list the causes of losses within the harvesting and post-harvesting stages of the crop; the list above may help as a checklist. Ask them to rank the causes within each stage, then, having done that, to rank the two stages. If the rankings of four or five different informants or focus groups are similar, you can be reasonably confident that the main local causes of harvest and post-harvest losses have been identified.

improvements. A common investment mistake of this sort has been prefabricated silos, brought in with the idea that storage losses result from inadequate containers. But where storage losses are caused by problems in harvesting, threshing and winnowing (e.g. inadequate drying, soil contamination, infestation) as well as poor management of the stored grain (e.g. inadequate fumigation and turnover), silos alone can not necessarily reduce storage losses.

In general, small, low-cost innovations are likely to be the most effective means of reducing storage and other post-harvest losses. These might include improved crop drying, improved threshing floors, muzzling oxen (where they are used for threshing) and improved sieves. Traditional clay-lined baskets and, in dry areas, underground stores, when used with appropriate fumigation, can be quite satisfactory means of storage.

On-farm storage has declined in recent years
The decline of local storage, particularly on-farm storage, may be a natural consequence of economic development and the increased integration of the district into the wider economy, since trade takes the place of storage. On-farm storage is usually much less important and prevalent in accessible areas than it is in remote rural areas. In the Horn of Africa, for example, much of which is rural and remote, it is estimated that there is more grain held on-farm than in all other grain stocks combined.

On the other hand, decline of on-farm storage may be the result of long-term decline in crop production in the district, or, in the short term, the result of drought or other disruption of production, meaning that there is less surplus being produced.

In all cases, a long-term decline in on-farm storage is not necessarily caused by on-farm storage difficulties and is not necessarily a problem in itself. A sharp drop in on-farm stocks in an area that relies heavily upon them for its food supplies is, of course, an important danger sign for food security indicating crop failure, either in the most recent season or in successive seasons. As described in more detail in Chapter 10, which deals with drought preparedness, individual farm visits are needed to obtain a quick impression of the state of on-farm stocks. Such visits should be used to compare current levels with what stocks should be in that season and to establish how long current stocks will last.

Processing problems

Processing is a problem: grain mills are inaccessible and expensive
Lack of locally available grain mills has been a frequent problem in remoter rural areas, with a gap between often inaccessible large-scale mills, through which only quite large consignments of grain can be processed, and labour-intensive hand pounding. In recent years, small-scale low-cost hand- or diesel-driven mills have been widely adopted, in Botswana and Kenya for example. If these are not locally available, Intermediate Technology can be contacted for advice through the publishers of this book.

Farmers complain that local food habits are shifting away from traditional foods. Is there no possibility of improving the processing and presentation of local foods to make them more attractive to consumers?
Urbanization, rising incomes and subsidized imports of wheat and rice have cut into the markets for traditional foods, particularly where diets have been mainly sorghum, millet and cassava based. In general, preferred urban and higher income foods are meat, dairy products, wheat and rice based dishes and fast foods. Long preparation and cooking time, the tendency for urban and higher income people to consume wheat and rice based products, overvalued exchange rates and food aid making imports cheaper and more widely available, together with the limited possibilities for

farmers in low rainfall areas to switch to higher value grains – all these factors have made difficulties for sorghum, millet and cassava farmers in areas formerly reliant on these foods. The Sahel, Horn of Africa and West and North Africa are the most heavily affected areas. To a lesser extent the same is true of maize based economies (e.g. in East and Southern Africa and Latin America) where wheat and rice have made inroads into food markets at the expense of maize products.

Removing the subsidization of food imports (often on wheat and rice) and assisting farmers to switch to higher value activities (such as livestock and tree products) are important in this situation. But there is also room for improving the market for traditional foods by improving their processing (to reduce the preparation time for traditional dishes), creating new 'fast' recipes using these foods and improving their packaging and presentation. A simple start may be in introducing milled and packaged sorghum, millet and cassava flour into urban markets and supermarkets. In Botswana this has proved most popular with consumers, with growing demand for sorghum flour.

This problem of loss of markets for traditional foods usually occurs in accessible rather than remote rural areas, since they are more subject to urban influences.

Suggested interventions include:

○ Carry out an informal market survey among traders and consumers to see whether there is an unsatisfied demand for packaged and more easily available flour from traditional grains.
○ Encouraging the preparation of attractive snack foods, such as biscuits, galettes, pancakes, pies, crisps, from the local traditional grains. These may provide the basis for a small employment-generation project among women (see Chapter 4), if the market is promising. A key consideration will be the regular availability of the traditional grains or root crops at attractive prices.

Summary

1. The roles of the state and the private sector should be and can be complementary and mutually reinforcing in making food markets work better.
2. In general, for food markets to function well support from the state is required. Firstly, the state should improve market infrastructure and competition; secondly, it should prevent market failure through being able to supply food in an emergency. In general, the more efficiently the market works and the less the risk of market failure, the less intervention is required from the state.
3. The use of simple techniques of analysis and quick methods of collecting

information can go a long way towards an understanding of the overall workings of the food market, where the main problem areas are, and what are likely to be appropriate interventions by government.
4. In deciding priorities for action it is useful to begin with a summary analysis (Box 4.4) of government activities and regulations as they affect local food markets.

CHAPTER 5
Creating Incomes and Employment

Unemployment and low incomes are pervasive local development problems. In most cases the rural manager has to rely on central government or NGOs to put income-generating projects into operation. But there is a key local role both in suggesting, initiating and reporting on projects, and in creating a local environment favourable to employment and income generation. This chapter looks first at the changing nature of the rural unemployment and low income problem and the reasons for public sector intervention, then turns to what can be done to improve the economic environment in order to encourage employment and income generation for the poor ('indirect measures'). A discussion follows concerning the 'direct measures' that can be used to generate incomes, plus a troubleshooting guide to some of the problems that may arise.

The changing rural employment problem

The overall trend of change in rural areas is towards more people becoming dependent on off-farm incomes, whether locally or further afield (see Chapter 2). There is greater involvement in long distance travelling for work, more petty manufacturing and service occupations and relatively fewer agricultural jobs. An important implication is that increases and decreases in off-farm employment and self-employment opportunities are becoming the factor most affecting rural incomes.

Within this changing structure, policies and projects to increase local income generation, particularly off-farm, have gained in importance as a means of reducing poverty. The rural poor typically lack either the farm assets to generate sufficient income (e.g. productive land, livestock), or the employable family members to find work of sufficient quality or quantity on- or off-farm, or they lack the funds, skills and opportunities for running their own business.

Why should government and NGOs be involved in trying to raise and maintain people's incomes?

Economic theory suggests that unemployment may be *structural* or *frictional* in nature. Structural unemployment is long-term, whereas frictional unemployment is only temporary, as people can move between jobs, altering their occupations and skills quite quickly to adjust to the changing economy. Except in the case of seasonal unemployment, the unemployment in rural areas (particularly remote ones) is mostly structural, as people have fewer chances of shifting quickly to alternative work.

A principal reason for unemployment or underemployment of resources, including labour, is the presence of market imperfections (i.e. blockages) that obstruct the buying and selling of the resource. Imperfections include both man-made ones, such as excessive taxes or obstructive regulations, high minimum wages, or sheer bureaucratic inefficiency, and also those resulting from natural obstacles to communication, transport and movement of people. Imperfections raise costs, reduce profits, discourage investment and ultimately hinder the regaining of skills and assets by the poor.

A further cause of unemployment and underemployment of resources is economic change itself. New markets, new production techniques and shifts of population always cause some unemployment as people are displaced from old occupations; these changes do not always create new employment opportunities as rapidly.

Improving transport and communications, reducing administrative obstacles and enabling the poor to get assets (land, finance, skills) with which to respond to changing market opportunities, together create a more conducive economic environment for private investment and chances for the poor to establish new livelihoods. The public sector and NGOs are essential in both tasks. Firstly, they should help to protect legally and actually the assets of the ordinary person and the community (a major task in the early stages of development in a rural area, when the rich and powerful are eager to obtain and exploit land, mines and forests cheaply, and when the desperately poverty stricken may be stripping the soil of vegetation). Secondly, they should assist the poor to participate in the income earning opportunities that changes in the market economy offer.

In summary, the role of the public sector and voluntary organizations in promoting people's income earning opportunities is threefold:

1. To assist in protecting assets (both legally and actually).
2. To reduce market imperfections by removing barriers against investment and employment, and improving transport and communications.
3. To help poor people to gain assets with which they can create their own incomes or find employment in the changing economy.

Carrying out this role involves both *indirect measures* that serve to create an environment which promotes sustainable production, trade and employment, and *direct measures* which create incomes immediately for people by providing them with productive assets or access to wage employment.

Indirect measures: creating an environment that fosters productive employment for the poor

Although direct measures, discussed in the next section, provide an immediate means of raising the incomes of the food insecure, indirect measures which preserve assets and make the economic environment more conducive to income generation are an essential first step, without which direct measures may easily fail. Furthermore, direct measures are expensive and have their limits. Creating the conditions for asset preservation and retention and reducing the economic obstacles in the way of income generation and employment creation can make a far larger long-term contribution.

Creating the conditions for asset preservation and retention

The state has a unique responsibility for the preservation of natural assets. Much grazing land, forest and wildlife and many deserts and water sources are resources traditionally owned communally, now usually by the state with local government responsible for their maintenance.

The state also has a responsibility for enabling the poor, as far as possible, to retain their assets, since they risk destitution if they lose them. Livestock and arable land are particularly at risk. A major finding of research on rural food security (notably Sen 1981) is that loss of assets is a threat to rural food security for two reasons. Firstly, loss of private assets (livestock, land, implements, house, cash) moves a rural family from being poor to being food insecure. Secondly, food insecure rural households in different parts of the world depend heavily on common resources for survival, particularly during periods of stress, such as droughts. Such families may use common grazing more intensively, collect wild fruit and roots, cut trees for firewood and charcoal burning, and fish more intensively. Depletion or loss of access to these common assets removes an important fall-back income source.

The local state, with its politicians and departments, co-ordinated by the administration, has a legal, mediating and planning role in protecting and preserving assets, which no non-state organization can take on. Local NGOs have a responsibility to press the state to carry out its role fully and fairly.

Legal role

Many countries which formerly were colonies had strictly enforced rules in their colonial days regarding soil and forest conservation. Often these rules were unpopular with local people and, after independence, were relaxed to varying degrees either legislatively or simply by no longer being enforced. Kenya, Zimbabwe and Malawi were all in this position.

Legislating effectively to preserve rural assets is extremely difficult. The difficulties are both in framing the legislation (What should be conserved? where? What levels of use of soil, common grazing lands, natural forests, rivers and lakes are sustainable?) and in enforcing what may be unpopular laws. The interest of the individual in conservation is almost inevitably less than that of society as a whole, since individuals see their own small use of common resources as being of minor cost to the environment.

The way forward is to rely not only on laws which in many countries have become virtually unenforceable but also on action based on what might be called the principle of conservation in conditions of increasing resource scarcity: *natural resources are only conserved when they can be used profitably and controlled by small groups or by individuals*. In other words, in the battle to survive and to profit, people value and maintain only those resources which are productive, and whose product they can rely on for themselves in the future, confident that in the meantime others will not have used them up.

Practically, this means ownership and control by an identifiable individual or group with a clear interest in maintaining the resource. The most difficult resources to conserve are wildlife, natural forests and wetland habitats – all of which have resources that are easily destroyed for quick profit. The task is to turn these resources to profitable use *while conserving them in their natural form*. Tourism, community benefits from wildlife management (as in Zimbabwe's 'Campfire' scheme) and natural research can all be paying propositions – and will be increasingly so as international pressures for conservation increases.

Information role
Lack of reliable information on the state of the environment and the causes of degradation is a major obstacle to progress in conservation. Local managers can promote research to increase understanding by identifying environmental issues on which more information is needed and encouraging publicity of local environmental problems.

Mediating role
The local state can bring together views and initiate consultations on what are essentially common problems.

Planning role
Priority must be given to key local resource conservation issues in investment decisions. The problem up to now has been that rural resource preservation has had no political constituency backing it and no powerful local interests behind it. Wherever this is the case, it is an indication of tenure problems or a lack of voice for those who suffer from the loss of their assets.

Reducing the obstacles in the economic environment to income and employment generation
The obstacles in the economic environment are both *material* and *administrative*. The material obstacles that rural areas suffer from include high local business costs (transport, staff, power, materials, spares), small markets and lack of experienced entrepreneurs. Improvements in

Box 5.1 *Income generation audit: does government hinder or help locally?*

The purpose is to check through, with the help of the local public and media, the state and parastatal activities which affect income generation and employment, in order to identify in what ways state regulations, taxation and services, help or hinder income and employment generation.

1. List the activities of government that affect production and business locally. Check the following list for questions and issues:
   o agricultural extension: who does it reach, does it help?
   o land allocation and distribution: is it done quickly, does it favour production, employment?
   o licences and permits:
      mining
      forests
      manufacturing
      trading
      moving food and produce
   o building regulations: are they practical and appropriate to local conditions or do they hinder necessary construction?
   o employment regulations
   o police services: do they provide security to people and business premises?
   o local taxation: who does it fall upon and does it discourage production and employment?
   o infrastructure: how adequate is the provision of roads, schools, and market services?
   o investment: does government encourage new entrants, particularly small business, to invest and provide competition to local monopolies; does government encourage or discourage minority groups to invest and carry on production and employment locally?
2. Carry out some informal interviews with local business people – small, medium and large – going through the list with them. Invite the local chamber of commerce, and any local small business associations or clubs (e.g. savings clubs, farmers' clubs, women's associations) to respond and speak up on how government helps or hinders their activities, and their suggestions for improvement.
3. Discuss the results locally in meetings with government, local politicians, local press and radio.

A public audit of the effect of the local state on income generation and employment can obviously be quite controversial, particularly when it leads to allegations of corruption or incompetence or issues to do with land. A few tips:

o keep the focus on the issue of income and employment generation
o separate issues of major controversy out for further enquiry to enable the discussion to return to the main issue
o encourage participation as much as possible, particularly independent press and radio: they are the administrator's best ally and most able defence in dealing with matters of the public economic good.

infrastructure (roads, communications, market facilities, finance) reduce business costs and are the main focus for government planning and economic development activities. The administrative obstacles are government regulations and practices which raise costs to local businesses and discourage local investment. These may include licensing (where it restricts business), building regulations, excessive minimum wages, restrictions on movement of goods, excessive taxation (particularly if the tax is a substantial share of income or produce, which may discourage extra effort) and inefficiency, delays, obstruction and corruption.

Material obstacles are only gradually removed, as a result of public investment and increased economic development. But local administrative obstacles are potentially more quickly reduced, provided they can be properly identified, the effects of reducing or removing them can be worked out, and local political and higher level government support can be obtained. An informal public audit of government practices and regulations as they affect employment creation and income generation may be a useful exercise. See Box 5.1 for ideas on how you can go about this.

Direct measures to raise incomes

Direct measures to raise the incomes of the poor consist of income-generating programmes which promote self-employment by providing households with productive assets, and employment creation programmes, usually labour-intensive works programmes, which provide short-term employment for wages in cash and/or kind.

Income generation: promoting self-employment through asset creation
Income-generating projects are characterized by getting income-generating assets directly to the target group: these include land, training, and credit for working assets, such as livestock, vehicles and machines. They are distinguished from employment-generating projects, which are designed to increase wage employment by stimulating investment.

Income-generating projects cover a wide variety of assets, and require greatly differing levels of back-up by government and/or NGOs. The least demanding are those which require only finance; the most demanding require infrastructural investment and maintenance, and assistance with training and marketing.

While the earliest income-generating projects were in agriculture (e.g. settlement and irrigation schemes, ranching projects) the greatly increased interest in income-generating projects now focuses on small-scale manufacturing and services. This is the result of the mushrooming of the 'informal sector' around growing cities and even small rural towns, as the poor and unemployed seek to provide whatever goods or services they can to those with money.

There are broadly two different philosophies underlying management of income-generating projects, which might be called *minimalist* and *interventionist* (following the ideas of Remenyi 1991). The minimalist philosophy regards assistance beyond the minimum as counterproductive, leading to increased dependence by the poor on hand-outs. In practice the minimalist approach takes the form of assisting with credit provision to overcome the imperfections in the market for credit, i.e. the reluctance of banks to lend to the poor at market rates of interest. Beyond that, according to the minimalist approach, commercial conditions and relations should apply, since generally the poor themselves know what sort of market opportunities they can best exploit and, since they are expert at exploiting opportunities, the small investments they make usually yield well. Support can be provided mutually through groups of the poor, which can even provide much of the necessary funds through their savings.

The interventionist philosophy assumes the poor suffer from multiple forms of deprivation and require more substantial assistance. In practice it favours approaches with greater involvement by those managing the project (in selection of beneficiaries and activities) and the provision of finance on terms more favourable than commercial rates backed up with support services, such as training, marketing and supplies.

A clear issue in planning income-generating projects designed to raise the incomes of the food insecure is whether a minimalist approach – which obviously is easier to administer – can benefit the food insecure, who are by definition the poorest of the poor. Before discussing further the planning of income-generating projects (IGPs), a few words are necessary about the critical role of groups and co-operation among the poor in facilitating IGPs.

The importance of groups and co-operation among the poor
The process of economic change in rural areas makes the poor increasingly invisible, particularly the poorest who are the most food insecure. They tend to live away from the main roads, their voices are usually not heard at public meetings, and they take little part in the growing consumption- and media-oriented society. This is why the existence of group organization among the poor can be critical to the success of income-generating projects directed to them, in terms of:

- identifying who and where they are, what their needs are, what possibilities they have;
- deciding on suitable financing arrangements – groups make collective organization of savings and credit a possibility which can mean a quicker, more efficient and sustainable means of finance, since the work of government or the NGO is with the group, to whom individual beneficiaries are responsible.

But co-operation and group organization among the poor is not something that the manager can simply create. This is underlined by the adverse experience with top-down government-inspired rural marketing and consumer co-operative societies which in many cases ended up either going out of business or becoming virtually government run.

Group organization among the poor may already exist in one or another form, such as burial clubs or 'rotating fund' savings clubs (e.g. all members contribute equally weekly and each one receives the accumulated funds in turn every few months). To what extent existing groups have the potential to expand their activities into co-ordinating finance for income-generating projects in the group will always depend on many local, situational factors.

In general, groups function better the more they are:

o limited and specific in their objectives;
o relevant to their members' immediate needs;
o have members with similar needs, and who are similar to each other;
o know each other fairly well and depend on each other to a degree.

In practice this means small groups from particular localities. The credit groups for Grameen Bank projects in Bangladesh are no more than four or five in size, with all members having similar occupations (see page 71).

The key role of local women
A number of factors makes working with local women likely to be of critical importance in income-generating projects. First, in many countries, women are the most active in local voluntary groups, whether these are purely women's groups or mixed. Second, women often have the reputation among development managers of being more stable and reliable, specifically drinking less, and being more concerned to spend income earned directly on home and children. Third, female single parent households are often among the poorest. Fourth, increased income earning opportunities for women, as well as better education for women, are emerging increasingly as critical factors determining child health and family planning.

Types of income generating programmes
A large number of programmes in recent years, run by governments and by NGOs, have focused on providing loans to small-scale entrepreneurs to acquire working assets for petty manufacture, repair or service provision. Such assets include tools, machines, vehicles and dairy animals. The assumption behind such income-generating projects is that the poor, small entrepreneur cannot raise finance from the banks because he or she has no collateral security, while borrowing from a money lender makes the loan uneconomic because of the unreasonably high rates of interest charged. Thus viable small business ventures which would take place if the entrepreneur could borrow at market rates are not made. This is the

rationale from the 'minimalist' standpoint discussed above; the 'interventionist' view would assume that the small entrepreneur probably faces other obstacles as well (such as lack of technical and organizational skills) which require further intervention by the public sector or NGOs.

A recent survey of NGO-run credit-based IGPs classifies them into three broad types (Remenyi 1991). The first is the *pure credit* type, in which the purpose is simply to get credit at commercial rates of interest to the micro-entrepreneurs, on the basis of personal integrity (in the case of individual loans) or by lending via an association, or via a board of responsible local individuals – who in both cases take responsibility for the loan. The approach is deliberately minimalist: beyond supplying credit, the NGO does not get involved in the business venture in any way, leaving it completely up to the entrepreneur. A second approach is *welfare oriented* which adopts a wider interventionist role, concerning itself with assessment of the venture, provision of training, infrastructure and perhaps inputs. This approach is more in the manner of the community oriented integrated development schemes.

A third approach is the *savings-linked* approach, involving a local savings club which lends to cohesive groups who accept joint responsibility for the repayment of loans. It is different from the first two approaches in that the loanable funds are provided by the target group themselves, instead of coming from the NGO's own finances, or being on-lent from a bank or donor via the NGO. The savings-linked approach is used by the Grameen Bank in Bangladesh:

> All lending by Grameen is done through its groups of landless poor. Each group consists of five persons, each of whom shares a common socio-economic situation and similar aspirations. Each group must be reasonably homogeneous in its occupational membership; . . . a group has to meet specified criteria before it is accepted into the Grameen circle, which is done with considerable ceremony to mark the event as a significant achievement (Remenyi, 1991: 79).

Because most of the small investments made are highly profitable the Grameen Bank has been able to operate on a completely commercial basis.

An additional category of IGPs – the largest in terms of sheer quantity of financial assistance provided – are the *public sector programmes*, such as India's 'Integrated Rural Development Programme' (IRDP), and Botswana's 'Financial Assistance Programme' (FAP). They are characterized by close involvement of government from the central level, which provides (or guarantees) the funds and sets up the programme administration, to the local level, which assesses business proposals, oversees selection of beneficiaries, payment and repayment of funds, provides back-up support to entrepreneurs, and monitors the programme. Compared to even the most interventionist 'welfare oriented' NGO approaches, public sector programmes are larger (usually covering the whole country), tend to be more 'top-down' in their planning and administration, and are probably a lot more expensive per loan, given the extent of administration involved.

Public sector programmes often have a larger grant element than do NGO programmes. Botswana's FAP is based entirely on grants, which saves on administrative costs (since finance becomes a one-off transaction without loan servicing) but increases disbursements per person assisted. India's IRDP uses a combination of grant and loan through subsidizing the interest rate charged.

Selection of beneficiaries

Issues include who and how to select, and by whom the selection should be made. Given that self-targeting of the poorest (see Chapter 2) is not possible in asset creation programmes, two different approaches, or a combination of them, can be used. The first is the **personal approach**, identifying food insecure people locally and the assets they could most suitably use to improve their incomes. The opposite is a **self-application approach**, putting word out widely about the nature of the programmes, what is being offered, and inviting applications. Advice and help can be provided with filling in applications, which can also be screened to some extent to try to direct the assistance to the needy. The approach taken will obviously depend on the local circumstances. Key questions in making the decision will be:

o *Are the needy already employed, or self-employed, in activities in which the acquisition of complementary assets can improve their income?* If so, less attention might be needed in seeking out new activities which they can take up i.e. a more indirect approach to their problems may be appropriate. If not, as in the case of displaced people who have lost their means of livelihood, what they need in order to provide livelihoods for themselves may be less clear.

o *Are the needy part of a fairly cohesive social structure, through which they can be identified?* This might be more likely in rural than in urban areas, since traditional village structures may still be in existence. A personal approach, either through village structures (as in India's IRDP) or by using participatory appraisal (see Appendix I) may then be appropriate.

o *Is there a substantial risk that a self-application approach will result in the funds not going to the target group?* In general, the more indirect the approach and the larger the grant element in the assistance, the more likely it is that entrepreneurs who are not from the target group will attempt to share in the benefits. This is less a problem for deliberately broad-based income-generating projects but a real problem where benefits are to be focused onto the food insecure. Botswana's broad-based FAP has small-, medium- and large-scale facilities, all with incentives to generate employment, with larger grant elements for the more disadvantaged households (low income, single parent household, remote area).

On the other hand India's IRDP is specifically focused on benefiting the poor, with much of the disagreement regarding its level of effectiveness focused on how many of the households it assists are poor in the first place.

○ *Should the projects be directed specifically to women?* In many poor communities there is sense in directing local IGPs more towards women. Single female-headed households are a feature of the 'culture of poverty'[1] which establishes itself in urban slums particularly, with women bearing more of the burden of both providing for and rearing children, while men are more footloose – many work and live away, with home ties more to their own mother than to particular women with whom they cohabit temporarily.

More of women's than of men's earnings may go towards food and essentials for children and women may have more active and stable co-operating groups: this is a critical feature which may make the difference between success and failure in income-generating projects for the poor, as discussed above.

Which types of activities are likely to be the most successful?
This section looks at what makes a micro IGP succeed and then presents an overview of a range of IGP activities.

Critical factors in making a successful micro IGP are:

○ *an accessible market* – ideally nearby, strong, reliable
○ *available inputs* – reliable supplies and prices, particularly the critical higher technology inputs which may be essential for more specialized activities, e.g. chemicals, veterinary services and supplies, supplies of inoculated chicks for raising broilers, supplies of fingerlings for pisciculture
○ *familiarity with the materials, techniques and products* – people should ideally be taking up activities with which they are familiar or which are simple to learn
○ *motivation to produce and sell* – without motivation the project cannot succeed; some of the food insecure will lack motivation, through lack of confidence or disability.

Hundreds of different IGP activities have been promoted in numerous different schemes. Box 5.2 lists a selection of the activities promoted in India's IRDP and Botswana's FAP.

As the list suggests, the distinguishing characteristics of IGPs are their smallness and low start-up costs. Most are in the tertiary (i.e. services) sector. Some of these have agricultural links, but most are related to people's consumption needs – underlining the reliance of IGPs on the urban informal sector. In general, the easiest IGPs to set up (requiring minute start-up capital and virtually no skills) are in very small-scale retailing. But for the same reason these fail very easily because of market saturation.

Box 5.2 *A selection of income-generating projects promoted by India's IRDP and Botswana's FAP*

1. Primary sector

Seed production and marketing
Fruit tree nursery
Training and pruning of fruit trees
Gardening and flower growing
Mushroom production
Fish culture in freshwater ponds and lakes
Fish seed production and rearing
Fish and prawn cultivation in brackish water areas
Fish and prawn seed collection
Honey processing
Cultivation of medicinal herbs and plants
Poultry
Piggery
Sheep and goat rearing
Bee keeping
Minor irrigation

2. Secondary sector

Agriculturally linked:

Processing cereals and pulses
Processing, preserving and canning of fruit and vegetables
Bakery and confectionery

Other:

Cottage match production
Fireworks manufacture
Non-edible oils and soap production
Leather products
Pottery
Handmade paper
Palm based products
Forest products: e.g. gum resin
Handicrafts and handloom weaving
Coir products
Flaying, curing and tanning of animal hides
Silk spinning and weaving
Limestone, lime shell and products
Household utensils manufacture, of aluminium, wood and iron
Bamboo and cane industry

3. Tertiary sector (services)

Agriculturally linked:

Supply of inputs (seeds, fertilizers, pesticides, etc.)
Supply, repair and maintenance of agricultural and irrigation equipment

Digging and boring of wells and tubewells
Laying and lining of irrigation channels and pipes
Collection, storage and marketing of agricultural and horticultural produce

Linked to animal husbandry:

Artificial insemination and basic veterinary services
Supply of fodder and feed
Sale of milk and milk products
Collection, storage and marketing of eggs, meat, hides, skins and bones

Linked to sericulture:

Supply of silkworm eggs
Collection, storage and marketing of cocoons

Linked to forestry:

Supply of seeds, seedlings, plants and saplings
Collection, storage and marketing of forestry produce

Linked to fisheries:

Supply of fingerlings, feed, etc.
Collection, storage and marketing of fish and products
Supply and repair of nets

Linked to village manufacturing:

Repair and maintenance related to carpentry and blacksmithing, household machinery (radios, watches, electrical appliances, cycles, vehicles, stoves, sewing machines, etc.)
Installation, repair and maintenance of biogas plants
Collection of manure and other raw material for biogas plants

Linked to construction:

Masons, plumbers, carpenters, blacksmiths, electricians, etc.

Linked to transport:

Operation, repair and maintenance of:
   animal drawn carts, cycle-rickshaws, hand carts, vans and boats (co-operative basis only)

Retail:

Agency work on behalf of artisans
Any small-turnover retail venture
Fair price shops (i.e. shops through which price controlled basic foods are sold and rationed)

Banking and insurance:

Collection agents for banks and insurance companies

Entertainment:

Circulating libraries
Hifi equipment
Bands

Estimating the success of an IGP
An IGP is successful if it benefits the target group and is sustainable.

Benefits to the target group
Benefits of IGPs to the target group are usually assessed by:

o comparing the recipients' new income level with what they earned before taking up the project
o establishing the extent to which the beneficiaries of assistance do actually fall within the target group.

Evaluations of benefits under India's IRDP try to do both of these by calculating recipients' incomes before and after receiving their finance, to assess whether they should actually have been eligible for finance in the first place (which they should not have been if their initial incomes were above the determined poverty line) and to assess whether the asset they received has had the effect of raising their income above the poverty line. On this basis there has been much criticism of IRDP for too often missing its target group, i.e. too many of its beneficiaries have had incomes above the poverty line in the first place.

But the difficulty of assessing people's incomes should not be underestimated, and the methods used in some Indian IRDP evaluations are open to criticism on this score.[2] Income measurement problems include:

o Relying on beneficiaries' recall, since written records are rarely available.
o Poor people usually have multiple occupations, mostly seasonal or otherwise variable through any year: without regular visits throughout the year, noting down their earnings, it is difficult to get an estimate with any accuracy.
o The income of the whole household is difficult to ascertain from questioning one member only: women's and men's income sources may differ and they may only have a hazy idea of what the other earns.
o Valuing consumption from own production (e.g. food production) may be difficult.
o The poor are no more keen than any one else to disclose their income (even if they know it, which they probably do not with any accuracy) unless doing so will bring some gain.

Household expenditure can be somewhat more easily and reliably calculated. But some of the same problems of multiple and variable expenditure by different household members arise. The household will need to keep a record, and several visits will be required through the course of a year in order to get a good estimate of annual household expenditure (see Casley and Kumar 1987:134).

But before you give up in despair over the difficulty of assessing a beneficiary's income or expenditure, focusing on the sustainability of an IGP provides a useful framework for assessing its impact, avoiding the measurement of overall household income and expenditure, while focusing attention on particular benefits or difficulties that the IGP has brought to the household.

Sustainability

As with any private business venture the basic measure of success of an IGP is whether it remains in business without subsidy, thereby providing a sustainable income to the beneficiary. Sustainability depends partly on profitability (i.e. profit as a percentage of the value of the investment) since the higher the profit the more worthwhile it is for the household to give up other activities in order to make a success of the new business. This is especially important for peasant households where activities and income tend to be diverse. But, as discussed above, profitability is not the only factor determining the success of an IGP. Sustainability of an IGP is increased if it is:

○ profitable
○ convenient (proximity, familiarity of tasks)
○ simple
○ labour saving
○ a ready source of quick cash with only intermittent labour
○ not dependent on expensive and locally scarce, non-renewable inputs.

Assessing likely sustainability of an IGP to the household involves estimating the net financial benefit to the household of taking on the IGP by subtracting the additional costs of the project (including any cost of diverting labour or resources from other activities) from the additional income that it brings in. It is also necessary to establish if the household is encountering bottlenecks in running their IGP. Box 5.3 provides an example of assessing likely sustainability. The profit calculation is based on the 'partial budgeting' technique used by farmers for making quick calculations of whether to substitute one crop for another on part of the farm. A standard budget for that type of IGP locally may be used, if available, for checking the listed inputs and costs. The result tells you whether the IGP has benefited the household or not. It even allows a ranking of different potential IGPs for a household, according to their net financial benefit.

Finally, it must be remembered that the IGP programme as a whole might have some negative impact on incomes of non-beneficiaries who were already running small businesses of the types promoted for the poor by the IGPs. This happened in the first years of Botswana's Financial Assistance Policy in the case of small manufacturers of cement blocks in villages, where subsidies to new producers led to oversupply in some cases. Where this happens the programme is difficult to justify and is on very uncertain political ground. These 'backwash' effects are less:

> **Box 5.3** *Quick assessment of the sustainability of a household income generating project*
>
> **Situation:** Mary Khotse is a widow with three young children, her oldest daughter being eight years old. She has a small rainfed farm, growing one crop of maize, sorghum, beans and melons per year. There are no other adults in the household; she gets occasional help in the agricultural season from her brother. She formerly did part-time labouring to provide cash. She received a loan a year ago, under an income creation scheme, to invest in a small diesel hammer mill, and now does service milling of grain in her village.
>
> The mill has a capacity of 1.6 ton of grain per day, but she has been milling about 1 ton per day over half the year. One advantage of the new business is that she no longer has to travel away from home for casual labouring and this has enabled her to spend more time in her own fields, thereby decreasing the amount of grain she needs to buy for family consumption.
>
> **Task:** To assess how sustainable the new source of income is.
>
> **Net financial benefits** (Pula):
>
> **COSTS**
>
> *Revenue lost:*
> Wages from casual labour: 0.5 per hour × 8 hours, 180 days per year
> Total   720.00
>
> *Costs added:*
> Running costs of mill: daily, for milling 1 ton of grain.
> Variable:
> diesel, 1 litre/hour @ 0.45/litre × 8 hours   3.60
> oil, 0.2 litres @ 1.25/litre   0.25
> Fixed:
> depreciation   1.29
> maintenance @ 225/year and 180 days/year   1.25
> Total daily running costs   6.39
> Annual running costs, operating 180 days/year   1 150.20

- the greater is the local deficit in the product
- the more the programme enables the substitution of local production for imports
- the more the programme enables the poor to produce for their own consumption, e.g. food growing and processing
- the more agriculturally related the production
- the more the production is destined for export markets.

Principles in designing income generating projects

Although IGPs require detailed planning of finance and technical inputs, the principles on which their design rests are simple:

Loan interest and repayment @ 1 000/year for three years	1 000.00
Total annual costs, operating 180 days per year	2 150.20

BENEFITS

Costs reduced:

Travelling costs for casual labour 0.5 × 180 days per year	90.00
Purchasing of grain for family consumption, 50 kg @ 0.40	20.00
Total	110.00

Revenue added:

Revenue for daily milling 1.0 ton of grain: 1 000 kg × 0.03/kg	30.00
Total revenue, operating 180 days per year	5 400.00

NET FINANCIAL BENEFITS

Total annual benefits – total annual costs 110 + 5 400 –720 – 2 668.60	2 121.40

Non-financial benefits: More time spent with children at home, since the mill is at the home and Mary no longer travels away for casual labouring.

Main problems and prospects: Labour shortage: Mary is the only adult and children are too small to help. She is concerned that if she falls sick she may not earn enough to sustain her loan repayment. The labour shortage problem is particularly acute in the agricultural season when she needs to spend time on her own farm but is anxious that she will lose customers if unavailable to mill their grain. She may hire casual labour in the next agricultural season if the milling business remains good. Overall, she is pleased with the investment and will sustain it provided she can find suitable assistance in the agricultural season, which should be no problem at the level of profitability of the mill.

Source: The household is fictitious. The operating data for a small diesel hammer mill are adapted from Haggblade (1982).

1. Identify the beneficiaries

Who the intended beneficiaries are will determine the type of activities promoted and how they are promoted. Urban poor, small-scale farmers, landless labourers, pastoralists each have different skills, preferences and living environments.

2. Build IGPs on the resource base of the area

IGP projects should be oriented to existing and planned infrastructure in the area, thereby reducing their costs and building local linkages. An example from many Indian districts is the linking of the Indian IRDP's dairy cattle distribution component to the massive investments in providing a dairying infrastructure (veterinary, co-operatives for collection, processing and storage). Poor people receiving one or two dairy animals under the scheme can only use these viably for generating cash where there is an established dairying infrastructure in the neighbourhood.

The approach to IGPs that will tend to emerge from using the local resource base as a guide is one of looking to new infrastructure investments to provide some component, large or small, of income generation for the poor, through:

o *Local sourcing* – new ventures, e.g. mines, plantations, irrigation works, award supply contracts in their construction phase and beyond. Efforts to assist local small businesses to be competitive in competing for these contracts against larger contractors from further afield include ensuring that supply contracts are put out to competitive tender, that local businesses are aware of them and are able to tender for them.
o *Attaching an income generation component* – specifically designing in a component of the investment for local small-scale income generation. Examples: in road building, supplies of aggregate; in irrigation schemes, microplots for the poor; in afforestation, small-scale nurseries. This can and should be done on a commercially viable basis, not as an act of charity.

3. Wherever possible go for the easiest, most readily undertaken activities, producing goods and services locally in short supply

These are activities which the beneficiaries can begin virtually immediately and presently do not undertake through lack of capital to obtain the tools, equipment or supplies of raw materials or semi-finished goods. The beneficiaries themselves are the best guide to such opportunities locally.

Labour-intensive employment schemes: lessons and guidelines

Labour-intensive works (LIWs) have become an increasingly important initiative in many low income countries because of:

o *An increasing capital/labour price ratio*, which is a result of their changing relative scarcities as population has increased and capital become more scarce.
o *Growing unemployment and vulnerability*, rural and urban, with seasonal unemployment and vulnerability of incomes to drought in rural areas.
o *Lack of or deterioration in infrastructure*, including roads, dams, buildings, fields, water supplies, irrigation, sewerage, pavements, retaining walls, contour bunds, forests, rubbish tips, windbreaks.

LIWs generally have a favourable ratio of economic and social benefits to costs.

Benefits include (actual and possible):

- They provide incomes.
- They are flexible: can relatively easily and quickly be expanded or contracted to provide more or fewer incomes to create additional employment seasonally or to counter income and asset losses through drought.
- They can decrease drought susceptibility.
- They can improve infrastructure, and thereby raise future income.
- They can be 'self-targeting' to the poor, i.e. only those most in need will want to work on them if wages are sufficiently low.

Costs include (actual and possible):

- They require planning, finance, management and engineering expertise (to varying degrees, depending on the project).
- They may compete with peak agricultural labour requirements if put on at the wrong time of the year, and thereby decrease food production.
- Financially they can be a high-cost, low quality method of providing infrastructure if poorly managed.
- They may be seen as a demeaning form of relief by people who are not accustomed to earning a living from manual labour.
- They cannot solve major rural unemployment problems and might be used as a palliative while little is done to reduce structural unemployment.

Management issues

The issues that arise in setting up, running and monitoring rural labour intensive works schemes can be grouped into managerial and technical. These are looked at below, followed by a brief step-by-step guide to initiating and running LIWs.

The managerial tasks span the planning and design, day to day running, relations with employees, politicians and community, central government and NGOs (if involved). The following are some of the main management issues that arise, arranged in question and answer format.

What are the objectives?

A key but neglected question is which objectives the labour intensive works scheme is supposed to fulfil. The easy answer is that it should provide *both* incomes and useful public assets. But in practice these two objectives are not always immediately realizable: providing quick employment may mean rough and ready 'make work' projects of little real usefulness. It may even mean no projects at all as the administration resorts to food distribution, as in Kordofan and Darfur provinces of Sudan in the 1984–5 drought. Figure 5.1 sets out the trade-offs between simple and more complex projects, and the preparation period required to get them going ('slow start-up, quick start-up').

Works projects which are both labour intensive and turn out substantial additions to rural infrastructure, such as irrigation channels, dams, bridges

```
                    Complex project
                          |
                          |
                          |
   Slow start-up    4  |  1      Quick start-up
   ─────────────────────┼─────────────────────
                    3  |  2
                          |
                          |
                          |
                    Simple project
```

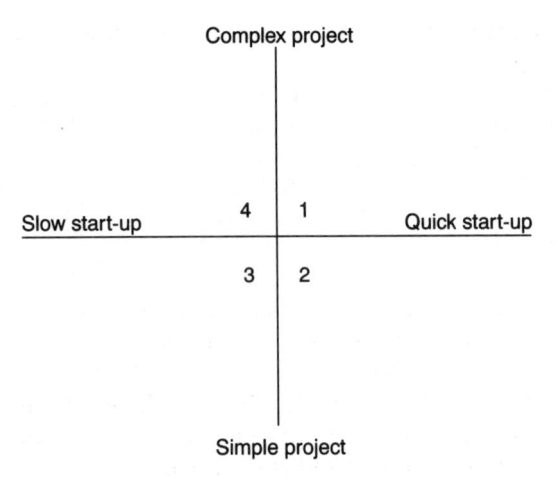

Figure 5.1   *Trade-offs in works projects*

and water piping, require some engineering expertise and technical supervision. They must also be appropriate to users and be maintained. Setting such projects in motion quickly requires experience, technical skills, good management, planning and consultation. Examples of where this has been done can be taken from the Indian states of Gujarat and Maharashtra. Dams and irrigation channels are locally designed and built through labour-intensive schemes, and can be started up within days as required. A stock of prepared projects is available, together with supplies of materials and tools, and the technical expertise needed to run them. In Figure 5.1 they fall into quadrant 1. In less favourable circumstances, projects which need to be started up quickly to provide employment are of necessity simple, requiring little planning and few tools, such as clearing, gathering or breaking stones. These fall into quadrant 2. In still less favourable circumstances, where administration is severely run down, even such simple tasks may be difficult to start up which implies a quadrant 3 situation. Where there is not the necessary experience, organization and funds, mounting more complex works projects necessarily means a slow start-up time, as indicated in quadrant 4.

The implication is that a rural local administration or NGO, which may be called upon to run labour intensive works projects, needs to decide its priorities: whether to be able to mount labour intensive projects at short notice or only with delays; whether the projects are to be of the simplest type or more substantial. The compromise that is possible and suitable will depend on local circumstances, most particularly what needs to be done locally to improve rural infrastructure. For example, in the Ethiopian highlands, erosion control through constructing contour bunds has provided a project that is substantial, and yet is fairly easy technically to plan and supervise, thereby achieving a high proportion of unskilled labour costs in total costs.

How can conflicting objectives between beneficiaries, government and funding agencies be minimized?
Conflicting objectives have been a major weakness in LIW programmes, especially where government is relatively weak, or even divided, or where an authoritarian approach is adopted towards the target group of envisaged beneficiaries. Under these circumstances local people may feel more or less forced into co-operating with a government-led project, just to 'please the minister' even where they are doubtful about its advantages. Their real opinion of the project – and therefore their actual extent of co-operation – remains hidden. This is a sure recipe for disaster, but is all too frequently found in rural areas where administrators, more often senior ones, see their role as dictating to local people to 'enlighten them'.

Maximum consultation with the target group – setting aside romantic notions of rural social harmony, establishing who the potential projects will really benefit, jointly deciding on a project which will *most benefit and most involve* the specific target group – is the way towards reducing conflicts over objectives and preparing the ground for a worthwhile project.

Conflicting objectives may also arise between governments and funding agencies. Weak governments may make undertakings which they cannot fulfil, in terms of counterparts, supplying local management and covering local costs, as a survey of the ILO experience indicates (Gaude *et al.* 1987). Inexperienced donors may try to push for unattainable levels of commitment by government to the programme.

How to ensure there are enough people who will offer labour, and how to make sure that the poorest people get the work?
A great advantage of LIWs is that they automatically target the poorest people, provided that the pay rates set are low enough. The issues involved in setting pay rates are discussed below. In general, the rates of pay determine the turnout for work but close attention needs to be paid to designing the size and timing of the LIWs according to labour availability so as not to decrease labour inputs.

Who should run the schemes?
The practice is generally that they are run either by a separate unit set up for the purpose, within a local government department, or in some cases as a parastatal, virtually independent of local government; or that they are run by one or more government departments; or that they are contracted out to a private firm or firms, a practice much more likely for urban than rural projects.

In states where local government is weak and run down there has been a tendency for donors promoting labour-intensive works to by-pass government departments in the hope of getting the scheme to work more rapidly and efficiently; thus specialized units for running the works are sometimes set up (as in some cases in Sudan), often employing civil servants with substantial supplementation of pay. In these circumstances the NGO itself tends to be thrust into the leadership role, technically, organizationally and financially.

There are problems with this government by-pass model, because:

- It is short term in orientation, neglecting the fact that government will ultimately be responsible for running and maintaining the assets created (unless they are privately owned, e.g. farmers' fields).
- It can further undermine government locally by removing some of its best staff and creating an alternative, foreign-funded locus of decision-making in infrastructure creation and maintenance.

These problems can be partially overcome by having a controlling local committee for the projects, chaired by the local administration, including community representatives. But with day-to-day technical, managerial and financial administration controlled by the unit, the committee may easily become a rubber stamp.

But all the above options for control are superior to the worst case, where there is no one department or unit which is ultimately responsible for running or co-ordinating the programme, or where some technical departments oppose the programme (as in ILO's special works programme in Rwanda in the early 1980s) (Gaude et al. 1987:441).

The type of project determines who should be involved in designing it and carrying it out. Thus an afforestation project must involve the local forestry department in design and implementation, more especially since afforestation requires careful ongoing maintenance.

Variations are possible and common: in most cases the projects are formally run by government locally, with a varying degree of outside technical and managerial assistance. External financial assistance is the rule rather than the exception.

But sight must not be lost of the purpose of management: to run the projects so that useful assets are created and income is generated for the poor. If local government and line departments are very weak locally, a specialized semi-independent unit may be necessary, despite the extra expense and disadvantages.

Is it possible for local government to initiate and manage labour-intensive works schemes?

Labour-intensive works are one of the oldest administrative responses to hardship wherever the population is settled, used by emirates in North Africa, Pharaohs in Egypt and sultans in Asia. With modern local administrations now bound into wider, more centralized structures, and with labour-intensive works now frequently externally funded by international organizations such as ILO, WFP, FAO, UNDP and USAID, the initiation and execution of larger projects typically involves decisions at many levels.

However, the role of local politicians and development managers remains critical in initiating and promoting schemes. Scarce resources nationally and internationally mean that districts from which the most articulate and well-supported demands for assistance come, and which can convince central government and donors of their seriousness and ability to manage projects, are the ones most likely to attract development funds.

In poorer countries rural local government development budgets are generally so tight that they cannot fund additional works schemes. But they can:

o do much of the project preparation themselves, which helps greatly in raising finance, since they are then requesting funds for specific projects
o manage them themselves, particularly if in planning the budget for the projects (see below) allowance is made for bringing technical assistance into the department (foreign volunteers may be the most inexpensive source of skills, and have the additional advantage of providing on-the-job training).

The three key tips for local government in initiating LIWs that they will be managing themselves are:

o *Keep them small* – small projects have much more flexibility in stopping, starting and adjusting when the inevitable logistical delays arise (e.g. delays in funding, late arrival of equipment or materials, bad weather, etc.) and are more easily supervised and managed. Experience indicates that materials, finance and supervision are the most important resources for running rural works. Inadequacies in these three resources often cause the typical problems of delays in work and payment, poor work norms and low quality of work. Small projects minimize these.
o *They should preferably be productive infrastructure, with the benefits accruing as specifically as possible to the target group*: following this principle helps to reduce the most thorny management difficulties, i.e. motivating the workforce, pay levels, voluntary work, participation in decision-making, quality control, maintenance after completion.
o *They should not be too many or too dispersed* to make them manageable.

In the literature on famine prevention there is a debate over whether the successful provision of LIWs by local governments in well-managed states of India can be replicated elsewhere. The argument hinges on the capacity of local administrations to manage the projects. But the difficulty that local administrations have may be not so much their lack of capacity – since resources for LIWs can be relatively easily obtained – as their lack of experience and confidence in organizing and running LIWs: a situation in which a motivated administrator can make a considerable contribution.

> **Box 5.4** *Donors and NGOs funding labour-intensive works projects in Africa in 1990*
>
> *Multilateral donors:*
>
> European Union
> FAO
> ILO
> UNDP
> World Bank
> WFP
>
> *Bilateral donors:*
>
> Australia
> Canada
> Denmark
> France
> Germany
> Japan
> Norway
>
> *NGOs:*
>
> CARE
> LWF
>
> *Source:* Von Braun *et al.* (1991)

Should an NGO be invited to come in and run LIWs? Which NGO should be invited and how should they be contacted? To what extent should the NGO running the scheme be independent of government – should it set up an effectively independent unit to run them?

With the increasing use of labour-intensive works schemes in rural and urban areas of poorer countries it is very likely that one or more projects are or have recently been running in your country or even in your region. World Food Programme and ILO have the most experience with designing and assessing projects, while many different multilateral and bilateral donors fund them. Box 5.4 provides a list of donors funding labour-intensive works projects in several African countries in 1990.

While NGOs can provide technical assistance and finance, they work under agreement with central government. Working out such agreements may take time and can make for a rather top-down process from the capital to the regions and districts. However necessary this may be, especially for large programmes, its negative effects (inappropriate local projects, inadequate consultation with beneficiaries) can be reduced by initial project preparation at the local level.

Some countries (e.g. Botswana, India, Zimbabwe) have extensive experience with funding and managing LIWs themselves. In Botswana's case the

Food Resources Department in the Ministry of Local Government is responsible, while in Zimbabwe local and provincial government deals with the Grain Marketing Board.

At the end of the project who is to be responsible for the ongoing maintenance and for restarting the project, or others, if circumstances demand?

This is a vital question, particularly in the case of projects which require ongoing regular attention in operating and/or maintenance, if they are to be successful. Failure of works schemes occurs mostly because of inappropriate design, use and maintenance. These include irrigation works, water supplies, afforestation and gardens, all of which require careful consultation with and involvement of users and government departments in the design, implementation and maintenance. The general rule is that projects which create productive infrastructure for and with the target group beneficiaries have fewest maintenance problems, since the users will be motivated and able to maintain them.

How should the schemes relate to local communities and their leaders?

High levels of participation are essential in selecting projects, deciding on pay levels and work norms, organizing voluntary labour (where appropriate) and deciding on the target group who are primarily to benefit. As expanded below, high levels of participation are one important means of avoiding conflicting objectives between managers and target group. Studies have found that low participation is associated with lower motivation and greater misappropriation (Clay 1988:148) as well as poorer targeting (Singh 1990:Ch. 7).

The means of assuring greater participation – meetings, maximum local publicity, clear and specific proposals, local committees – all enable the details of the plans to be discussed and disputed, and compromises agreed upon. A particular issue that arises, notably with directly productive projects, is that of land ownership. Directly productive projects (e.g. irrigation) often take place on private land, meaning that the landowner or tenant gets the lion's share of the benefits. Ideally the landholders would themselves be the target group. But where not, arrangements regarding finance of the works are needed, such as half the costs of the works being supplied publicly with the other half covered by a loan.

Is it possible to manage rural works projects so that unskilled people acquire some skills from them?

LIWs are not designed with the purpose of achieving skill acquisition but to employ as many unskilled people as possible. However, projects which create new assets (forests, roads, irrigation) involve more skilled and semi-skilled work, create opportunities for informal training and learning and provide work experience.

Is it possible to run rural works schemes on which people are paid, together with community development type schemes in which people contribute voluntary labour?
Kenya runs both LIW projects on which people are paid and *Harambee* community projects on which people work voluntarily. These two modes have been combined elsewhere (e.g. Botswana, Uganda). Running the two side by side obviously requires great care in discussing with the local community the nature of the projects, times of year when they are to be run, who will benefit from them, etc. There is no simple formula that always applies. In general, the more substantially a project benefits a particular, readily identifiable and limited group of people, the more likely it is that they will contribute labour free of charge at off-peak times in its construction and maintenance.

LIWs designed to create or replace poor people's incomes are, therefore, only likely to be able to combine paid with voluntary labour where the particular group of poor people who self-select themselves to work are the principal beneficiaries. In reality, as Gaude et al. (1987:433) point out in reviewing the ILO experience, it may be that '. . . this is a political choice which is the sole responsibility of the national authorities'.

The pay on LIWs is sometimes in the form of cash, sometimes in food. Does it matter which?
Cash and food (including cooked meals) are the usual form of pay on LIWs, often a combination of the two. Generally, cash is much easier to manage than food since storage, transport, perishability and local appropriateness problems are avoided. But the form of payment is less important than paying punctually, fairly and conveniently. The payments system is the focus of corruption in LIW management through fictitious workers, inflated days worked and straightforward misappropriation. Separating the payment department from the technical management of the LIWs, and instituting spot checks by an auditor on the accounts of both, are usual arrangements for reducing graft.

If the payment is to be in the form of food aid from abroad, special care is needed in order to ensure that the food is appropriate to local tastes, delivered in good time (food aid is all too frequently delayed at ports) and not brought in in such large quantities that it reduces food prices so much as to discourage farmers from production. Where possible, it is usually preferable to receive local grain instead, if central government is willing and able to make the exchange (an arrangement that is known in food aid jargon as 'local purchases'). A further decision which may be required is whether to sell the food aid in local markets and use the proceeds (the 'counterpart funds') as payment on LIWs, or use the food itself as the means of payment. The trade-off here is between ease of management (it is often easier to sell the food aid than store and transport it) and loss of value, since the food itself may be more valuable to the LIW workers, and they could in any case sell it if they wished.

How will the works fit into infrastructure planning in general in the district?
Works that produce roads, divert rivers or streams or put up buildings for schools or clinics obviously need to be linked into the wider planning of roads, watershed development and health and education provision in the district. Since the majority of productive rural works involve waterworks (check dams, percolation dams, irrigation channels) the adoption of the watershed as the basic planning unit is sensible. This approach is used in the Employment Guarantee Scheme in Maharashtra, India (Singh 1990: 269), allowing development priorities for the watershed and the interests of upstream and downstream users to be taken into account.

Summary

1. Unemployment is a growing problem in rural areas and structural change in agriculture means that employment opportunities must increasingly be found in non-agricultural production and in services.
2. The role of the public sector in promoting people's income earning opportunities is to assist in protecting the assets of the poor (both legally and actually), to make markets work better by removing barriers which hinder investment and employment, and to help poor people to gain assets with which they can create their own incomes or find employment in the changing economy. Carrying out an informal audit of government practices and regulations as they affect local employment and income generation is suggested.
3. Efforts to raise incomes and employment are both direct and indirect. Indirect measures improve the economic environment by reducing costs and obstacles to production and trade. Direct measures are targeted to the poor and consist of:
   (a) Income-generating projects (IGPs) which rely on provision of assets to raise income from self-employment. Approaches underlying IGPs are 'minimalist' or 'interventionist' in tendency. Success depends on accessible markets, available inputs, familiarity with materials, techniques and products and the motivation to produce and sell.
   (b) Labour intensive works projects (LIWs), designed to provide immediate, short-term benefit to the poor by increasing direct wage employment. Their advantage is that they are self-targeting to the poor. Guidelines for designing and running LIWs are indicated, as well as the trade-offs involved between size of projects, start-up time and necessary supervisory skills. The key rules for initiating and managing LIWs locally are: keep them small, few and not too dispersed, and ensure that the benefits of the assets produced are gained by the target group as directly as possible.

CHAPTER 6
Water

People's access to water in rural areas, and the price of water, affect their food security substantially for the following reasons.

o Rural water costs tend to be high and unstable, whether in cash terms or in the time and effort required by households to fetch water, thereby affecting their real incomes.
o Rural clean water sources are often vulnerable to drought and floods, causing increased costs of obtaining clean water to rise greatly at a time when food prices are also likely to be high.
o Water-related local diarrhoeal diseases reduce food absorption in infants, linked to local sanitation and personal hygiene problems.
o Access to water for livestock and crop irrigation is the gateway from poverty for many in rural areas.

This chapter discusses the three key food security problems to do with rural water management – vulnerability of supplies, links to diarrhoeal diseases and access by the poor to water for productive purposes. To introduce the topic, the rural water management problem is first set out, followed by a summary of the potential benefits of improved rural water supplies and of the conditions necessary for successful government–community co-operation in water management.

The rural water management problem

Provision of water supplies in rural areas has absorbed a major part of development and recurrent expenditure in the budgets of rural local authorities in poor countries. It is also an area that has suffered from poor planning and administration, in which net costs have often so greatly exceeded anticipated levels that water supplies have deteriorated.

There are a number of reasons why managing water supplies is a particular challenge for the rural manager:

o Rural water comes from multiple sources, often seasonally variable, hence it is difficult to predict fully the consequences of improving one or other source. In the words of the ODA's *Manual for the appraisal of rural water supplies*, 'Many rural water schemes fail either because the water provided is not used at all, or is used in a way which drastically reduces its potential benefits' (ODA 1985:Ch. 2).

o Water may be a prestige investment, since tangible and visible benefits can be delivered fairly quickly; thus local politicians are often keen on water improvement schemes, with the risk of political jealousies and intrigue over which village or neighbourhood gets priority in water improvement.

o Rural water planning, installation and maintenance does not always fall within the responsibility of any one department and therefore rather easily becomes the victim of interdepartmental inefficiencies. Often one department is responsible for well digging and equipping while another is responsible for maintenance.

o Maintenance has been a particular problem. This is more complex than it seems at first, since although many maintenance problems are the result of inadequate provision for maintenance (in terms of technical expertise, labour, organization, parts, funds) they can also be the result of poor design. The result may be water supplies that nobody wants to use because they are remote, or unreliable, or yield poor quality water, or because the maintenance costs of the inappropriate equipment installed is far above any possible capacity of the consumers or the local administration to pay. Thus a variety of planning and management problems produce the symptom of a system poorly maintained.

o Village communities are often expected to contribute to the costs of water improvement, but the limits of their contribution are often poorly understood which, as a result, may be poorly managed.

Potential benefits of improved water supplies

Figure 6.1 usefully summarizes the potential benefits of rural water improvements, stressing the other inputs that must be present if benefits are to be realizable.

Government–village partnership in water management

Before focusing on food security priorities in water management it is important to stress the basic role of government–village co-operation in rural water management, since community involvement is usually essential, particularly in remote areas, if the improved supply is to be maintained at reasonable cost.

Administrative models
Rural water supplies are administered on a centralized or a decentralized basis, or some combination of the two (Feacham *et al.* 1978). A centrally

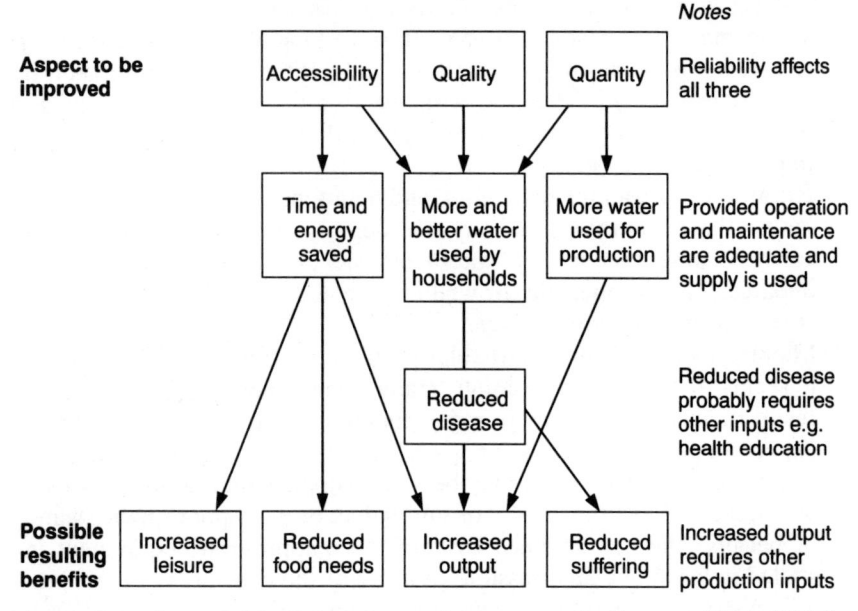

Aspect to be improved	Accessibility	Quality	Quantity	Notes: Reliability affects all three
	Time and energy saved	More and better water used by households	More water used for production	Provided operation and maintenance are adequate and supply is used
		Reduced disease		Reduced disease probably requires other inputs e.g. health education
Possible resulting benefits	Increased leisure	Reduced food needs	Increased output	Reduced suffering	Increased output requires other production inputs

Figure 6.1 *Potential benefits of a rural water supply. Source:* ODA (1985)

controlled agency or ministry is at the hub of the system, with a district or regional branch office essential if the system is to be more decentralized – especially where self-help from village communities is relied upon. Table 6.1 illustrates the distribution of administrative tasks between central authority, branch office and community in a shared responsibility model.

Role and limits of self-help
What can be achieved by community self-help and what cannot be achieved is often poorly understood. Assumptions are often wrong, as in the following examples:

Assumption 1: *'identification with the project is maximized the more the community contributes at all stages'.* The experience is that communities which have contributed labour for the construction of the supplies may be less rather than more enthusiastic about contributing further labour or funds for maintenance, feeling that they have made their contribution and the government should now take over. The Lesotho water improvement programme found that 'The community developers' ideal of community identification with the water supply can only be realized to the extent that the community identifies with the authority that provided it' (Feacham *et al.* 1978: 232).

Table 6.1 A compromise model: controlled self-help

Activity	Central authority	Branch office:* district or region	Community
Establish	Decide upon project selection criteria		
Plan	Obtain information, allocate resources to regions on priority grounds	Select suitable villages and invite them to apply for specified projects	Organize, but only proceed when invited
Fund	Disburse grants and donor funds	Collect self-help contributions, prepare project memoranda	Raise specific funds and labour on an agreed basis
Implement	Provide central technical advisory unit, purchase materials	Provide technical supervision	Contribute labour or pay for work as arranged
Maintain	Provide maintenance funds	Employ maintenance staff	Provide occasional labour or services of a volunteer, alert branch office when necessary

* A well staffed and well supported branch office is absolutely essential to this model.
Source: Feacham *et al.* (1978)

Assumption 2: *'community labour in assisting with the construction of the water system is a saving to the project'*. This is only true where the savings on labour are greater than the additional supervision costs incurred, which may not be the case where there is no local expertise.

Assumption 3: *'the government's task is to tell the community how to maintain the installed water system, after that it is the community's responsibility'*. Villages are not necessarily more socially harmonious than urban neighbourhoods. Groups may quickly fall out with each other over politics or sharing work and benefits of a scheme. Government needs to play an ongoing helping role in guiding the local organization, helping to solve problems and usually paying some portion of maintenance costs. Maintenance cannot be left to self-help alone.

Government's role in building sustained self-help in water management

The key to sustained and effective participation is 'a genuine partnership between government and village and a realistic assessment of which responsibilities can be handed to the village' (ibid, p.233). This involves two types of support by government:

1. Assistance and advice with forming and running village organizations (e.g. the water committee), training in problem solving and maintenance of equipment and help with solving ongoing technical and organizational problems.
2. Clear division of tasks between government and village, recognizing that there are some tasks that the village cannot undertake well. These may include financing spare parts, with the village raising the labour to install them, since collecting money in the village for repairs to communal facilities is a task that is often difficult and divisive.

Key food security issues involving water

Drought vulnerability

Along with food supplies and the means to buy them, the availability of drinking-water for people and livestock is the immediate concern in drought.

The usual pattern of rural water use in arid and semi-arid rural areas is to make use of seasonally abundant supplies (water in seasonal wells, streams and pans) by moving herds and agriculture further afield in the wet months, returning to the permanent water supplies in the dry months. In terms of water sources, the seasonal variation in water use amounts to using many, scattered sources in the wet season(s) and fewer in the dry season, usually more concentrated in the proximity of villages. In severe drought there may be more people and stock remaining at the permanent water points as seasonal supplies are reduced.

Thus the tasks facing the rural manager attempting to reduce the drought vulnerability of rural water supplies are:

o To ensure that permanent supplies can withstand the greater than usual stress that will be placed on them in drought (higher levels of use mean lower water tables).
o To strengthen key vulnerable sources to ensure that the people and activities which depend on them can continue as normally as possible (i.e. with as little displacement of people as possible due to water shortage).
o To anticipate impending water shortages in good time and put corrective measures in place.

If there is a history of drought-induced water difficulties in the district, with resort to expensive emergency solutions (like road transport of drinking-water in tankers and bowsers), while priorities for investment to prevent recurrence are unclear, a rapid 'vulnerability appraisal' with water users may be useful (see Box 6.1). This will not replace good hydrological information but can supplement it most usefully and provide an overall picture of needs, and how vulnerability of supply can be reduced.

Box 6.1 *Vulnerability mapping of water sources using participative appraisal*

Object: To establish which are the most critically drought-vulnerable water sources, and decide what should be done, and how, to make them less vulnerable or to supplement them.

Unit of investigation: The individual watershed (i.e. valley area, into which surface water and runoff collects and in which underground water is recharged) is the most suitable unit for a rural area which combines residential with agricultural and livestock use. In a single watershed the water supplies for these activities are probably drawing on the same groundwater supplies and needing to accommodate each other. Taking the watershed as the unit of investigation therefore builds in any local conflicts over water (e.g. between upstream and downstream users, domestic and livestock), bearing in mind that conflicts are more likely in times of shortage.

Technique: Invite key informants (from different user groups where appropriate, e.g. domestic, livestock, irrigation) to identify local water sources, their type, importance, use, to rank their reliability in times of drought (use a ranking matrix – see Appendix I), to identify the fall-back sources of water during drought, and to offer opinions as to what is needed to improve their drought reliability. A map with water sources marked on it, either an official map, or one constructed by the informants, can be used to mark the key water points. They can be annotated according to drought vulnerability and possibilities for improving or supplementing their yield.

Besides producing a quick overview of local water adequacy the discussion will also address, in a less threatening manner than direct questioning would, local conflicts over water and its management.

Key issues that might be included in the discussion:

o Which sources are most relied upon?
o How did local people cope during the last drought?
o Have any changes to the supplies been made since the last drought?

Options for improving supplies so that they are less drought-vulnerable may include:

o reserve boreholes
o well-deepening
o percolation dams (to slow runoff and increase absorption, thereby recharging local groundwater)
o private storage tanks and dams
o 'water harvesting' (stone bunds to improve absorption and reduce soil loss).

Improving water supplies through labour-intensive works, where possible, forms a link between employment generation during drought (or during seasonal slack times) and combating drought itself. Where appropriate, this possibility is offered by building percolation dams, digging and deepening wells, building contour bunds, as carried out now in many drought-vulnerable rural areas (e.g. in India, Ethiopia, Botswana). See Chapter 5.

Links between water supplies and malnutrition
Diarrhoeal diseases are a major cause of infant and child malnutrition and mortality in poorer countries. Chronic diarrhoea reduces the absorption of food and acute diarrhoea causes dehydration and ultimately death.

Diarrhoeal diseases are predominantly spread by faecal-oral transmission. This can take place through faecal contamination of drinking-water (defecation in or near rivers and wells, poorly sited pit latrines) or of food and utensils (poor personal hygiene of food preparers, poor domestic hygiene, flies bringing particles of faeces and settling on food and utensils) or of infants' and children's play areas (causing hand-mouth transmission).

The incidence of diarrhoeal diseases is often higher in the wet season, which can be due to one or a combination of the following factors: the longer survival of bacteria in warm, moist conditions; low seasonal nutritional status therefore lower resistance to infection (crops still growing, food having to be bought); washing of faecal material into water sources by runoff; high fly populations; less hygienic village environment.

Thus the channels of faecal-oral transmission are multiple. Given the prevalence of poor personal and environmental hygiene it is not surprising that studies comparing villages having clean, uncontaminated drinking water supplies, with others having relatively contaminated drinking water, most often do not show any difference in the incidence of diarrhoeal diseases (Feacham *et al.* 1978, Ch. 5).

The indication is that improving personal and environmental sanitation and infant nutrition (see Chapter 3: Nutrition, Health and Disease) are the priorities in reducing diarrhoeal diseases (and other water-borne diseases, such as cholera and typhoid) after which cleaner and more abundant water supplies may also play their part.

There is therefore no necessary and immediate connection between more and better water and lower disease incidence. There is even a risk that poorly managed improved water supplies may increase disease risk through providing breeding sites for flies and mosquitoes.

Access by the poor to water for productive purposes
There are two points of caution regarding expectations of the impact of water provision on the incomes of the poor.

Firstly, even where water is the main constraint on additional income-generating production, as in the cases of irrigation water for dryland farmers or stock watering points for livestock keepers in dry savannah land, the high investment costs (borehole/tubewell/deepwell, pump, fuel, channels) and the competition among farmers for limited water point sites, generally means that smaller farmers do not easily acquire these assets. Group formation among farmers, plus the institutional back-up (financial, technical, organizational) to give them a chance of succeeding, are the essential components. An example of relatively successful water group formation is the state-backed experiment in Bangladesh, aided by the NGO 'Proshika', with groups of the poor putting in and managing irrigation systems for local farmers (Wood and Palmer-Jones 1991). The conditions for successful group formation are discussed in Chapter 5.

Secondly, fetching water for the home is traditionally women's work, which is sometimes heavy and time consuming. A clear benefit of more accessible and reliable domestic water is that it frees women's time. While this is a benefit in itself, it must not be assumed that the time saved will automatically be used on productive work or better child care. It is often used for increased leisure, as was found in the Lesotho and Swaziland water improvement programmes (Feacham et al. 1978:187). As in the case of a cleaner water supply itself, other factors intervene and determine whether the better water supply improves health and food security. These factors include how readily and profitably the saved time can be used productively. For example, in the case of agriculture, extra time can be used productively during peak labour periods, such as weeding and harvesting, but not necessarily at other times. In the case of child care, local norms and the mother's level of education, rather than free time, determine strongly the standards she will try to maintain. In the case of attempts to stimulate new productive activity, availability of inputs, skills, and a readily accessible and attractive market are essential if poor households are to take up new activities.

Summary

1. The three key food security problems to do with rural water management are vulnerability of supplies, links to diarrhoeal diseases and access by the poor to water for productive purposes.
2. 'Vulnerability mapping' of water supplies using participative appraisal may be a useful approach to improvement in areas with high drought risk.
3. If improvements in the quality of water and people's access to it is to improve health and incomes it must be accompanied by improvements in local sanitation habits and personal hygiene, plus the means (markets, capital, skills) to use the saved labour time or water access for production.
4. Managing the improvement of rural water supplies is often difficult because supplies may be from multiple sources, they may be seasonally vulnerable, responsibility may be divided among government departments, resources to provide for maintenance may be a continual problem and the limits of community contribution may be poorly understood.
5. A partnership between government and village is needed in which government's role is assistance and advice with forming and running village organizations (e.g. the water committee), training in problem solving

and maintenance of equipment and help with solving ongoing technical and organizational problems. The basis is a clear division of tasks between government and village, recognizing that there are some tasks that the village cannot undertake alone.

CHAPTER 7
Livestock

The livelihoods of poor people in remote rural areas often depend heavily upon livestock – whether they are nomads, small-scale mixed farmers using livestock, or employees on ranches – since remote areas often consist of either arid or semi-arid land which cannot be cropped intensively, or of relatively inaccessible hill areas. These environments favour livestock production because there are fewer diseases, there is a varied diet from browse and grazing, and the land generates less income from arable farming.

The food security role of livestock in a remote rural area may be critical: because of people's income dependence on livestock, because livestock are relatively drought-resistant and because acquiring livestock is often the main means by which poorer people can escape food insecurity. Livestock as an asset are extremely versatile: they provide income in kind or in cash (meat, milk, blood, fuel), inputs to agriculture (draught, manure), capital appreciation (they grow, multiply, and their prices trend upwards over time, providing protection against inflation), they are mobile, and they absorb very little high-cost labour (they can be looked after most of the time by old people and children).

It is essential that the rural manager in a remote area understands the role of livestock and as far as possible enables livestock to play a positive role in promoting food security, rather than the seriously negative role which bad management of the livestock sector can inflict.

We look first at the management of the local livestock sector during drought and then turn to livestock development for food security. The emphasis is on large stock (e.g. cattle and camels) and small stock (e.g. sheep and goats), followed by some remarks at the end concerning poultry and fishery development.

Managing the local livestock sector during a drought

Good management of the local livestock sector during a drought helps to prevent drought becoming famine, while bad management actually increases the risk of famine.

Avoiding the price scissors
The main risk is the 'scissors' of grain and livestock prices which comes into action when drought hits.

Livestock are quite drought-resistant compared to most crops: a one-year drought often has little impact on livestock themselves with no marked increase in livestock mortality, since livestock can shift to browse when grass is scarce, and can often be moved further afield to less drought stricken areas. It is in the second or third year of drought that the shortage of sustenance becomes acute and owners find themselves desperately looking to sell animals.

But even a one-year drought results in increased sales of livestock in remote rural areas where poorer people are dependent on local grain supplies and derive their incomes mainly from agriculture. The reason is that drought causes grain shortages (the more widespread the drought the greater the shortage) which raises grain prices (dramatically, in the case of major droughts) and causes poor people to sell their assets (often mainly livestock) in order to survive.

In severe, prolonged drought, as in much of Africa in 1983–5, local livestock markets and grain markets reinforce each other in a 'price scissors' in which grain prices are pushed higher (as scarcity increases) and livestock prices lower as more and more livestock are offered for sale, because they cannot be kept alive and because grain prices are so high that people have to sell more livestock in order to afford the grain. Once the drought is over the 'scissors' move the other way: grain prices stabilize or fall, while livestock prices rise sharply as herders try to restock from supplies of livestock depleted by the drought. The losers are the poor – driven to sell their animals at the lowest prices during the drought and then faced with greatly increased prices when trying to restock after the drought. Their losses can be devastating, especially those of small herders who have less access to markets further afield, as in Darfur in 1984–5 (De Waal 1989:159–63). The grain–livestock 'price scissors' is depicted in Figure 7.1.

Preventing the 'scissors' of livestock and grain prices depends most importantly on ensuring adequate local grain supplies. This prevents exceptional grain price rises and reduces immediate survival-driven selling of livestock during minor droughts. Secondly, increased availability of fodder and increased livestock buying during a major drought are essential to reduce the severe falls and subsequent increases in livestock prices.

Since the methods for preventing destabilization of grain prices (i.e. greater than normal seasonal fluctuations) are dealt with in detail in Chapter 10, we concentrate here on how to prevent destabilization of livestock prices.

Understanding farmers' own strategies during drought
Assisting the livestock sector during drought depends upon understanding, and working with, farmers' and pastoralists' own drought strategies.

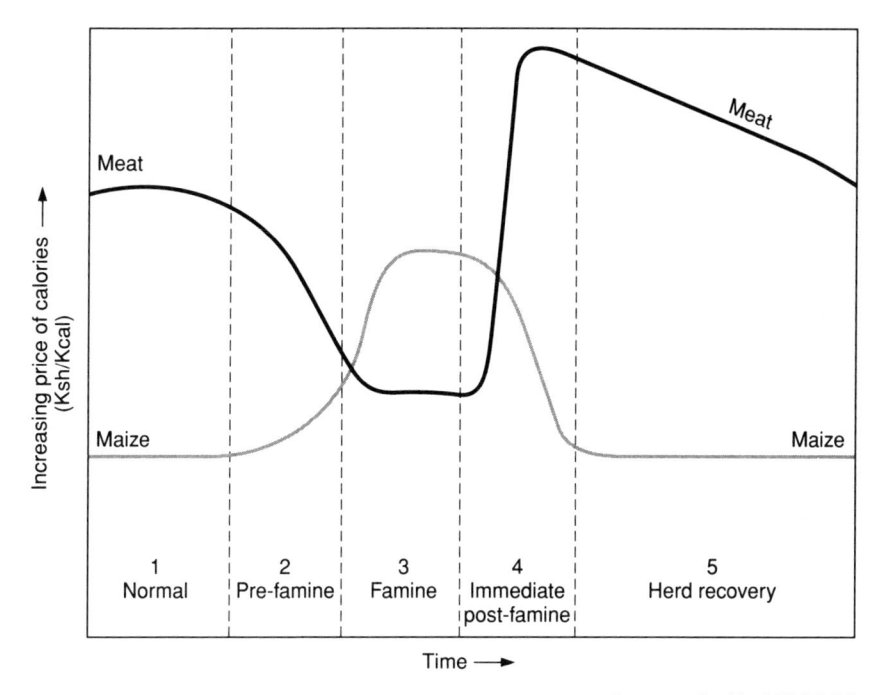

Source: Swift 1989:326

Figure 7.1 *The 'scissors' of livestock and grain prices*

Splitting the herd is the pastoralists' basic response to drought. Pastoralist systems and the livestock component in semi-arid farming systems are nomadic or semi-nomadic (transhumant), with seasonal movement of stock pursuing pasture and water. Drought changes the migration pattern as pastures cannot sustain the same numbers of livestock: more animals, particularly the breeding core, or 'milk herd' (breeding females and young) plus some oxen (for draught) may be kept near permanent water and towns, where feed can be obtained for them; the remainder of the herd (bulls, heifers, old cows, young males) may be sent much further afield than normal, possibly being 'loaned' to distant relatives, or split into smaller groups (if the herding labour is available) in a strategy of survival in which – during a major drought – only some will succeed.

Thus in Samburu district in Kenya in the drought of 1983–5, the Oxfam stock-buying campaign found that the animals available near the towns and villages were largely breeding animals (Downing *et al.* 1989).

Sell and keep is the drought strategy of more commercially minded livestock owners, particularly where grazing is private and drought reduces its stocking capacity. The breeding core is kept and surplus animals sold.

Many livestock systems, as in Botswana and Kenya, are a combination of pastoral and commercial, with the result that commercial incentives and livestock sales are not everywhere established. The result is herd build-ups during runs of good rainfall years and widespread stock deaths during major droughts: the grazing lands of eastern Botswana and western Sudan were littered with carcases during the great drought of 1984–5.

What can be done
The critical livestock policy objectives during major droughts in pastoral and semi-pastoral areas are:

○ To increase food grain and fodder supplies in the area.
○ To remove surplus stock.
○ To prevent people's incomes collapsing, so that they do not have to sell their core breeding stock in order to survive.

Emergency interventions

○ *Buying campaigns* by abattoir companies: difficult and expensive to organize in remote areas and fail if the buyers and transport turn up but surplus stock have migrated. They must take place in advance of migration with maximum information to livestock owners. Buying and holding in advance of transportation may be preferable where holding grounds are available.
○ *Local purchase, slaughtering and processing*, with meat sales and distribution to the needy, processing (drying and smoking of meat, grinding of bones for bonemeal, drying blood for blood meal and preserving hides). This may be much the simplest and quickest emergency means of increasing the market for surplus stock in an area remote from abattoirs and main buying centres, while at the same time making use of local skills and providing some needed temporary employment. The equipment required is simple: fires and cauldrons for boiling, barrels for meat smoking, lines and shade for meat drying, hand-operated grinders, chemicals for hide preservation, which may already be locally available. Drying and smoking make easy storage and transport possible. The key requirements are the resources to buy the stock and pay for the work to be done, the means to store and sell the produce, and care that the meat produced is not simply put up for sale at any price on the local market, since this will further depress meat and livestock prices; it can be distributed to the destitute (as in the Oxfam drought relief scheme in Samburu, Kenya, in 1984–5) who would not be buying meat anyway and may be very short of protein. In a drought-stricken remote area food grain is the key resource since it is in short supply in a drought, with high transport costs for bringing it into the area. The buying and processing operation can be carried out using livestock for grain swaps and food-for-work projects.

○ *Supplying fodder* will help to reduce livestock mortality and desperation sales but is costly (since fodder is scarce in droughts) and may be logistically difficult in remote areas. Special arrangements to bring in and distribute fodder are an essential component in drought management in Indian states such as Gujarat, where there is a high density of livestock (kept mainly for draught and milk) dependent on cultivated feed. But in remote, semi-arid areas where livestock density is low and animals forage on open grassland and forest, fodder provision is not usually practicable without considerable expense, except for the milk herd kept near the homestead.

Longer-term measures

○ *Restocking* projects are frequently run by NGOs, such as Unicef in Kordofan region, Sudan, and Oxfam in Samburu, Kenya, in 1984–5. They are asset distribution schemes designed to help rehabilitate those made destitute by the drought. Great care and consultation is required in selecting beneficiaries: they must be identified within the community as deserving and be able to care for the stock. Widows and single women with dependent children are typical recipients. The most appropriate animals for the scheme are pregnant females, so that the scheme can be run on a circulating loan basis, with the first female offspring used to repay the loan and redistributed to others in need. The chief disadvantage of restocking schemes is their initial cost since they generally have to buy animals in the immediate aftermath of droughts, when pregnant breeding stock sell at a heavy premium owing to their scarcity. They also require follow-up, as does any loan scheme, to ensure that the animals are not disposed of and that first offspring are returned. Restocking schemes are most easily run in conjunction with holding grounds which enable stock to be bought during the drought.

○ *Holding grounds* give greater flexibility in livestock policy. They take different forms – forests, parks, quarantine camps – but all are areas of grassland with low or zero stockholding, reserved for a particular purpose but which, in times of need, are potentially usable for temporary holding of livestock, the length of time depending on the grass and browse available. They are most effective in supporting buying campaigns, since they enable the stock to be gathered and kept in advance of transport or local slaughter, and also for restocking projects since they allow buying early in the drought when prices are low (thereby also supporting livestock prices) and redistribution after the drought when prices are high.

○ A *drought preparedness plan* in high famine risk remote areas is essential and is discussed in more detail in Chapter 10. The livestock component may appropriately include:

- sites for simple slaughtering and processing at appropriate points in the district: water, shade, concrete slab, basic tanning facilities;
- arrangements to use reserved areas as holding grounds in times of need, so that their normal use is adjusted to leave sufficient biomass for this purpose;
- specifying the tasks of livestock department personnel in good time (i.e. reporting excessive livestock movement, disease outbreaks related to nutrition, sales of breeding stock) and in dealing with emergencies once they arise (e.g. sales, disease control, holding ground operations, release from routine departmental obligations);
- procedures for running restocking schemes, with finance and management pre-arranged with appropriate NGOs – since state finance is usually too limited to sponsor restocking.

Managing livestock development to promote food security: Dos and Don'ts

Increasing the benefits from livestock production, use and trade through improved husbandry techniques, organization, and improved quality and quantity of livestock products is referred to as livestock development. In the modern world it mainly takes the form of technological improvement in breeds, feeds, medicines, management and marketing for higher productivity in animals (i.e. faster growth rates, higher reproduction rates, faster sales, and lower transport and marketing costs). These have enabled greatly increased production and lower food prices in many countries. But usually they have been accompanied by social change, particularly the amalgamation of farms into increasingly larger units.

Livestock development in lower income countries has often been a controversial and highly politicized matter – particularly in remote rural areas where livestock owners are nomadic or semi-nomadic pastoralists, and where 'self-allocation' and even fencing of common land by rich individuals may be occurring. Livestock development schemes with high level backing in the national government, supported by the World Bank (which mounted many such programmes in the 1970s and 1980s), may have been attempted locally, possibly with a ranch component.

There is now much experience with livestock development in lower income countries. Some Dos and Don'ts can be listed briefly:

Range-based livestock raising

- Recognize that range land has multiple users and enclosure (fencing) of range land will exclude the poor who use it for gathering or seasonal pasture. The livelihoods of the poor may be far more heavily dependent on access to these lands than is imagined, especially during drought when they are an important fall-back source of wild foods. Compensation is essential but may be difficult to arrange, particularly for the poorest, as the experience of Botswana indicates with the creation of fenced ranches under the Tribal Grazing Lands policy. Arranging compensation in the form of alternative land for settled users who are displaced is easier than for semi-nomadic and hunter-gatherer users who do not have definite land rights, even when they may be the ones who lose most heavily. Using participative investigation techniques (see Appendix I) is essential in exploring compensation questions.

- Beware of livestock development schemes which rely on quick improvements in herd productivity for their acceptability. Quick improvements are unlikely, either in traditional or more commercialized range-based livestock raising.
- Be especially wary of schemes which impose changes in social institutions – such as instituting group ranches in communal livestock areas – and which expect productivity improvements to flow from them, as is sometimes expected of land tenure changes, e.g. allocating ranches under freehold or leasehold tenure and expecting herd management practices to change to a ranch-style basis.
- Beware of proposed schemes that make no allowance for drought and disease losses.
- Be cautious of assertions that traditional livestock raising practices are less productive and more damaging to the environment than ranch-style practices under the same circumstances. The evidence is that traditional systems may be as productive as commercial ones when all livestock products (including milk and draught) are taken into account, while proof of long-term range deterioration is notoriously difficult to obtain and, when obtained, to attribute to overgrazing. Overgrazing certainly reduces biomass in the long term but switching to ranch tenure does not necessarily reduce overgrazing.
- Use participatory investigation (e.g. preference mapping and ranking) to establish the needs and preferred innovations of livestock owners.
- Increasing the productivity of traditional livestock raising may most effectively be carried out by improving veterinary and marketing services to livestock owners (particularly to reduce calf mortality – often as high as 50 per cent – and to encourage earlier sale) and by improving access to fodder, most effectively through promoting the raising of fodder trees near the home.
- Livestock management innovations (rotational grazing systems, paddocking, controlled breeding season) will only be adopted in traditional livestock raising if they fit in with household survival strategies. In particular, if they demand more skilled or educated labour inputs without very greatly increased profitability they may not be adopted, especially if the household's employable labour is working in town with the livestock

left in the care of the old, very young or disabled. The reality is that under dryland conditions managerial innovations usually do not raise profits from small herds greatly or quickly. Subsidized fencing schemes may be popular, as the experience in Botswana both in ranching and communal areas indicates, but as a means of reducing herding labour requirements and to keep livestock out of crops, rather than for the managerial innovations (e.g. breeding, weaning, grazing rotation) that the project designers usually intend.
o Water is the key dryland constraint. Provision of water opens up previously dry areas to grazing. Subsidized water provision encourages overstocking, particularly when combined with open access to the grazing.

See Sandford 1983 for a survey of the experience in range-based cattle and small-stock development.

Dairying
The experience with dairy development among small farmers (e.g. in India and Kenya) indicates that dairying can be a ready source of additional income. But it depends critically on:

o *An accessible market and a dairying infrastructure* (collection, storage, processing, veterinary services). The infrastructure may be prohibitively expensive to provide, unless the market can carry the cost in the price. Most advantageous for dairy based poverty alleviation projects is where the infrastructural network is being established around a strong and growing market, as in the urban hinterlands of India, and individual small producers can be assisted at low cost to become suppliers.
o *Availability of feed.* Feed may be a problem, particularly for the very poor who have little if any land and may be relying on common land to collect fodder. Fodder trees grown near the home provide a valuable feed supplement.

In arid and semi-arid areas there is frequently a milk surplus in the wet season, when calving takes place, while milk is virtually unobtainable at other times. Some of the seasonal surplus may be turned into ghee (butter oil) and cheese in order to preserve it, more fresh milk is consumed in the diet and there may be some sale or exchange locally. It is noteworthy that any sales are almost invariably informal and local. Attempts to set up modern milk chains linked to pastoralists generally fail, the infrastructure costs being too high (meaning that the price that can be offered to the producer is too low relative to the local informal market) and the supplies of milk too seasonal and intermittent.[1] More promising means of raising incomes from livestock products may be improvements in the quality, presentation and marketing of traditional products (e.g. cheese making), and greater availability of fodder and livestock services (Sikana,

Kerven and Behnke 1993); but in each case there are not ready-made, universally applicable solutions, particularly for nomadic or semi-nomadic groups. Participative investigation is essential. Attention needs also to be paid to ensuring that child nutrition is not reduced by any changes in milk use.

Rabbits, pigs, poultry, bees and fish farming
Discussion of livestock development often tends to focus on herded animals. But as a means of generating incomes and supplementing proteins and minerals in the diet of disadvantaged households with little land, raising small animals near the home often has more potential than cattle, sheep or goats. Assessing its potential in the area must be a high priority in exploring ways to improve local food security. Beekeeping requires little labour, its products (honey and beeswax) are easily stored and transported and most areas with flowering plants and trees are suitable. Rabbits convert vegetable matter to meat efficiently and live off greens not consumed by humans; pigs too, if provided with small quantities of feed concentrate, convert inedible by-products of crops (e.g. stalks, cobs) into meat and manure. Poultry meat and eggs are among the most widely acceptable and digestible forms of protein. Fish farming can be carried out on even the smallest of scales and benefits from manure and crop wastes for fertilizing the ponds and providing supplementary feed.

All such raising of small animals requires sound technical advice, local sharing of ideas and experience and veterinary back-up. (See Oxfam 1985 and Heifer Project International 1986 for practical overviews of requirements for raising small livestock.)

Summary

1. Livestock are often important to food security in remote rural areas owing to their versatility and suitability for dry environments.
2. Good management of the local livestock sector during a drought helps to prevent drought becoming famine, while bad management actually increases the risk of famine.
3. The main risk is the 'scissors' of grain and livestock prices which comes into action when drought hits, sharply raising grain prices and sharply reducing livestock prices. Its effect is impoverishment of people desperate to obtain food and to sell their starving livestock. After the drought a reverse 'price scissors' occurs as herders attempt to restock with depleted livestock numbers. Preventing the 'scissors' depends most importantly on ensuring adequate local grain supplies, and on increased availability of fodder during a major drought. Emergency 'grain for livestock' exchanges can be targeted by area, while restocking assistance post-drought can be aimed at the most needy households.

4. The livestock component of the local drought preparedness plan should improve the functioning of local food and livestock markets (easier buying, selling, transporting) as well as providing for future emergencies (sites for simple slaughtering and processing, arrangements to use reserved areas as holding grounds, specifying the tasks of livestock department personnel in early warning and emergencies, procedures for running restocking schemes).
5. The problematic experience with livestock development programmes has taught several important lessons.
6. Raising small animals near the home (poultry, rabbits, pigs, bees, fish) often has potential for improving diets and incomes of poor households at relatively low cost.

CHAPTER 8
Finance for Local Food Security

Instead of mandating to lend to the rural poor, governments should create an environment under which such lending becomes a business proposition and attractive to financial agencies
(Padmanabhan 1988:112)

The local manager often feels confused, out of touch and powerless in matters of finance for rural development. Perhaps financial decisions are taken far away – at regional or central level – and with far too much delay; there may be local responsibility for ensuring that public money is well accounted for but often virtually no discretion over what it is spent on; policy-makers' attitudes towards local traders and money lenders may be confusing, one arguing that they are exploiters, another that they are the financial mainstay of the rural areas; attempts may have been made to attract banks to the rural areas but perhaps they have come reluctantly, do not seem to finance those most in need or fail to reinvest locally much of the savings deposited with them. Perhaps worst of all, the rural manager may feel caught in the middle helplessly between the faceless demands of the national financial system (state and private) and the pressing, often conflicting, needs of local people: rich and poor, women and men.

For some managers, the risks of being accused of favouring one or other group, perhaps even of corruption, is reason enough for staying well out of private sector financial matters locally. But in every local government system the administration influences local institutional behaviour and it is essential that managers understand the issues and possibilities for improvement.

The manager's first task is to learn how local financial markets are functioning, particularly with regard to the incomes of the poor. Thereafter she or he should try to remove obstacles blocking their better functioning. But a strong note of caution at the outset! Schemes to improve rural finance – particularly targeted credit to the poor – have a high mortality rate. Some important lessons learned are:

o Do not push credit towards the poor without first removing the constraints preventing profitable use of the credit.
o Do not promote production by the poor which risks reducing their food security.

- Do not undermine local financial institutions by forcing them to lend unprofitably.
- Do not place a long-term debt burden on the poor.
- Do encourage group formation among the poor for improving savings and to provide group indemnity for individual loans.

This chapter provides suggestions for assessing the local financial system and the position of the poor within it, for identifying obstacles (constraints) to productive use of funding and for improving financial relations with central government and donors. It also discusses how to improve local public sector project funding and management and provides a checklist against which the food security impact of investment projects can be assessed.

Assessing the local financial system as it affects the poor

Identifying the major features of the local financial system as it affects food security is an essential first step. The following can help in making a rapid appraisal:

First, *identify the local patterns of credit and savings of the poor*. The Table 8.1 summarizes some of the features of a local pattern of credit, using an example.

Savings form as essential a part of the picture as does credit. Where rural financial markets are poorly developed much of the savings of the poor will be held as hidden cash or put into valuable but unproductive objects (e.g. gold and jewellery). As financial markets develop, more productive (i.e. interest bearing) alternative forms for saving become available.

To fill in the overview table, interview local key informants from among the poor and individuals from the formal or informal sector who provide finance to them. The purpose is to get an overall view of what the poor use

Table 8.1 Sources and uses of finance: overview of local patterns of credit and savings among the poor

Example: Remote area, where the poor are dependent on strongly seasonal agriculture, with high drought risk and undeveloped formal financial markets.

Source of finance	Finance for: Consumption	Investment	Seasonal needs	Emergency
Own savings		Main		Some
Formal loans				
Informal loans	Main		Main	Main
Saving associations			Some	

Key: Main = main source of finance for that need
Some = some finance for that need from this source
Blank = unimportant

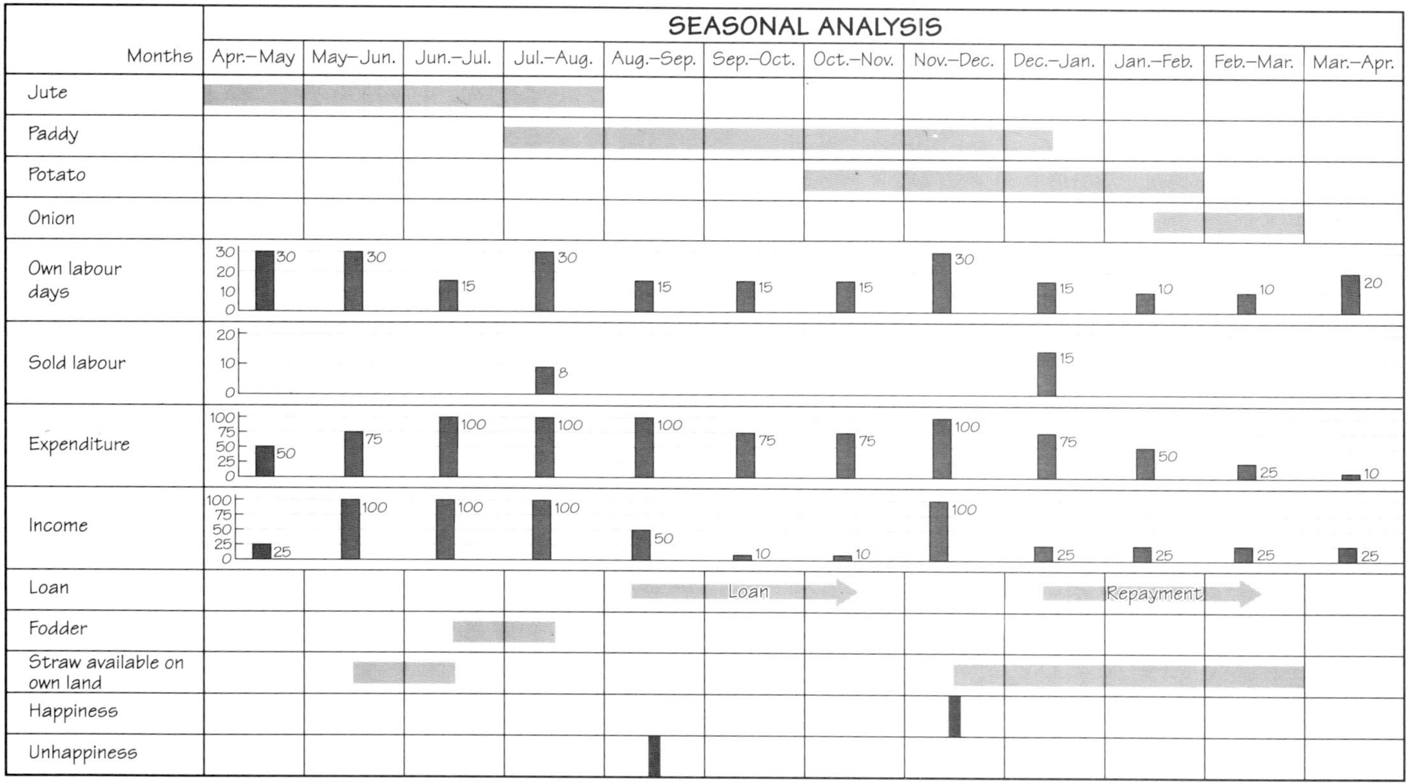

Figure 8.1 Using the seasonal calendar to understand money management among the poor

Source: IIED (1991) opposite page 100

finance for and of who supplies it, including use of their own savings. The table provides only qualitative information, i.e. only a picture of the types of finance used and who provides it, without any quantities. Its usefulness is in identifying the links between main types of financial need and sources. It can be as detailed as required. Separate tables for different groups among the poor should be drawn up if their credit and savings patterns differ substantially.

However, the overview table is summary and static and needs to be supplemented by using the seasonal calendar to explore how the poor manage their money: at which points in the year they have cash shortages and surpluses, their borrowing and saving habits. Many poor households in every society are caught in a vicious circle of cash shortage, debt, high-cost purchases and borrowing, and low value, emergency sales of labour and household assets. In the most depressed households this may be accompanied by poor management of money when the household does get it. Using the seasonal calendar in this way helps to identify the key financial problems of poor households (see Figure 8.1).

Observations to make from the seasonal calendar include:

○ Whether the households are heavily or continuously in debt;
○ Source of the debt;
○ Sales of produce:
  • is it sold in advance at low prices?
  • is it sold through the most direct channel?
○ If taking labouring jobs at time of most acute cash shortage is this depriving their own farm of labour when most required?
○ How the households manage their income when it comes in.

The purpose of the interviews with key informants is both to inform local policy and, more especially, to begin a dialogue with lenders and borrowers concerning possibilities for improvement in the system.

Second, *establish whether the constraints (blocks) on effective implementation of income-generating investments for the poor are financial.* This is particularly important, since one of the main weaknesses in rural development planning has been to assume too readily that finance is the key constraint, which once provided will remove others. The experience has been that it does not, with numerous failed rural finance projects to prove it: projects which cannot or do not repay their loans bankrupt development banks. A long debate has ensued over the role of government in financial markets. See the 'development' vs 'banking' approaches in Box 8.1.

Getting a rough idea of whether finance is a constraint on effectiveness of an income-generating project is less difficult than it might at first seem. Box 8.2 provides a checklist of steps and questions to work through with key informants among the poor and with lenders (informal and formal).

> **Box 8.1** *How much should government intervene in financial markets?*
>
> **The 'development school' vs the 'banking school'**
>
> The reluctance of commercial banks to lend to the poor, and particularly to farmers, has motivated many governments to force them do so, by nationalization in some cases. Targeted credit schemes, specifying the use to which credit is to be put, fixing rates of lending, operating through state owned development banks or with loan guarantees to private institutions, has been the style of the 'development school' of finance. It has much to show to its credit, particularly in agricultural infrastructure (such as water facilities, machinery, fences), but – argues the 'banking school' – at great cost in terms of bankrupt lending institutions, wasted money and failure to attract local savings as deposits which could then be lent for sound investments. There should be less intervention, more attention to providing the conditions under which financial institutions can succeed, and to removing the obstacles (such as inability to own land, inadequate marketing, infrastructure and training, and excessive regulations e.g. licences) which hinder poorer people from making their small businesses more profitable.
>
> There are now some points of agreement emerging, recognizing that governments have intervened excessively in the past at the expense of financial institutions and have pushed credit at the poor when it is not the main constraint; but also recognizing that commercial banks do not easily lend to the small business activities of the poor, that targeted grants can be a better vehicle for assisting agricultural investments (e.g. water, land) than subsidized credit, and that specialist financial institutions, which identify with the poor and involve a high degree of participation and group organization (Grameen Bank is a prominent example), have an important role to play in themselves, and as intermediaries between commercial banks and the poor.
>
> The debate between 'interventionist' and 'minimalist' approaches to assisting income generation among the poor (see Chapter 5, p. 63) is an extension of the 'development school' vs. 'banking school' approaches to credit.

Improving the local financial system for the poor

Some priorities for improvement will emerge from the quick assessment of patterns of credit and savings, and of constraints on expansion of small business activities for the poor.

If there are non-financial obstacles to expansion of small business and agricultural activities, such as regulations which restrict business, e.g. licences and controls, or land tenure restrictions, or very poor transport and communications, then reducing these must be the priority.

If finance for the poor seems the dominant constraint on small business opportunities for the poor, the reasons may either be the usual ones why formal financial institutions are reluctant to lend to the poor:

o high administrative costs per loan;
o no attachable assets to use as security;

Box 8.2 *Is finance a constraint or not?*

If there are other constraints blocking the successful participation in a business activity then additional finance may just be wasted. The following exercise with key informants, both borrowers and lenders, can help in finding out the constraints on expansion of local small business activity which exist and whether they can be relieved by finance:

- Trace through the stages of the industrial, agricultural or service activities that appear to be good candidates for expansion: the resources and production processes to be used, markets to be sold in, range of products, and risks. In the case of agricultural activities, the seasonal calendar will be a useful tool since the demands of the activity to be expanded are put into a time framework next to existing demands from other activities.
- For the same activities, carry out a brief preference ranking exercise (see Appendix I for guidance), asking the key informants to rank the activities in terms of profitability and riskiness, inputs availability, land, labour time, skills, marketing.

Some tips to be borne in mind on possible constraints:

Profitability and riskiness: If the activity is already widely carried out locally, using tried methods (e.g. chicken raising in an area where it is widely established), lack of profitability is probably not a constraint on further small investments, unless of course existing producers are going out of production. If it is a totally new activity in the area then risk of unprofitability is greater, and there is no substitute for a careful budget of costs and revenues, allowing for substantial variations and not forgetting to include family labour among the costs.

Inputs: Inputs may be a constraint if:

- the activity requires purchased inputs that are not locally available all year round
- prices or deliveries are uncertain
- the purchased inputs are essential and a significant proportion of costs.

Typical agricultural examples are fertilizers, pesticides, veterinary supplies.

Marketing: Marketing may be a constraint if:

- prices fluctuate widely
- marketing channels are uncertain.

Land: It can be surprisingly difficult to obtain land under suitable tenure arrangements for either agricultural or non-agricultural investments, particularly for the poor.

Labour: Shortage of labour is often a problem in income-generating activities hindering poor households from engaging in them, especially single mothers and old people. Clashes with other seasonal peaks in labour demand may occur (which should be observable from the seasonal calendar). Shortage of labour for working the household's land is a frequent complaint in small-scale agricultural development projects, typically where the employable members of the household are working away from the farm. But here the problem may actually be the poor productivity and profitability of agricultural activities compared to off-farm employment.

Technical and management skills: Where the activity is a new one locally or the household has little experience in it, technical and management skills may be lacking.

- poor funding proposals;
- better loan possibilities elsewhere, perhaps in urban areas.

Or there may be particular local reasons, such as where the poor group is an ethnic minority and there are language and cultural barriers to communication.

In either case the task for the public or NGO manager is the same: to improve communication, encourage constructive discussion of what may be a delicate local matter, and to understand the possibilities for improvement. There are generally two of these:

- Firstly, encourage banks to take a positive attitude towards reducing the obstacles in the way of their lending to small local business. This might include accepting charges over the assets bought as security rather than only land, preparedness to lend on a group indemnity basis to local NGOs and associations which themselves make individual small loans, simplifying loan application procedures, employing staff who speak the dialect of the poor and who involve themselves closely in the activities of the poor.
- Secondly, encourage group formation and local NGOs among the poor, such as savings clubs. These cannot be created in top-down fashion but assistance in forming and running them can be given. (See Chapter 5 for further discussion on group formation and income-generating projects.)

In addition, public sector loan programmes to farmers or small businesses are probably in existence in the district, have been previously tried, or are about to be tried again or expanded. The impact of these on the local financial system can easily be negative, given their often high rates of default on repayments and local controversies over who was or is to be awarded cheap loans and grants.

To get the most out of public sector finance programmes, both for the poor and the improvement of the local financial system, public sector programmes should:

- Make grants for capital items where there is great need and no realistic prospect of repayment, rather than use credit as disguised grants.
- Provide grants or credit only for investments in which the recipients themselves are investing their own savings.
- Keep the debt burden on the recipient small, manageable and short term.
- Take great care in the selection of beneficiaries of grants – where possible make it a participative process, so that there is public transparency and accountability in identifying who are the most deserving locally.
- Have any loan programme administered by local banks and NGOs who are developing their own credit programmes in the area and with the

groups concerned; support their capacity building through the programme and rather offer them incentives for good performance than guaranteeing cover for loan defaults.
○ Judge the programme by results (i.e. income generated, loan repayment, target group reached) rather than by loans and grants disbursed.

Improving project funding

In addition to improvements in the local financial system and the access that the poor have to it, there is usually need and room for improved project funding in rural areas, whether infrastructural or income generating, public sector or NGO. But improved project funding requires better overall project planning and management.

Weaknesses in project planning and management in rural areas include being too slow, non-participative, benefiting too few people, and failing to complete because money has run out.

The local manager can help to improve project planning, management and funding in the following ways.

Strengthening the local projects cycle: In most countries rural administrations manage the local end of public sector funded projects, within a project cycle laid down by central government (the cycle consisting of project identification, design, financial appraisal, implementation, monitoring and evaluation). Established NGOs often have similar practices. A frequent complaint is that the cycle is too slow, with too little local say in the final shape of projects. It can be improved, as was found in Kenya in the preparation of the District Focus programme in the early 1980s, by raising the skills and responsibilities of local development committees. This helps projects to be more speedily and participatively identified and screened, and proposals to go forward to central government in a more developed form (specified, costed, prioritized). Raising the performance of local development committees in this way usually requires training of officers, councillors and committee members.

The task of improving the local part of the projects cycle is made easier if there is a district planning process actively in place. A district development plan usually consists of:

1. A survey of the state of development in the district (by area and sector of the local economy).
2. A statement of priorities for improvement and resources available.
3. An investment plan, setting out the public sector investments to be undertaken in the period, their phasing, sequence and the resources they will employ.

Project selection is formalized in the plan's preparation and updating, with deadlines for submission and approval. Investment projects are identified (ideas collected and short-listed), designed (components and resources required), costed (financial costs and benefits specified), implemented, monitored and evaluated. District development committees usually set the local priorities, identify possible projects and carry out some of the basic design work, with more detailed design and costing being done by the central government ministry responsible, which also usually undertakes the implementation, monitoring and evaluation.

Screening projects for their impact upon local food security: An aid in screening local investment projects roughly but quickly for their likely impact upon local food security is provided in Table 8.2. Project implementation is divided into its three components of construction, operation and maintenance, with the various inputs to these (such as land, labour, transport, materials, water, fuelwood, finance) checked against components of the local food security system for possible beneficial or negative impact. The components of the investment project and the local food security system should be listed in as much detail as is required for the particular project. The purpose is to check through the impact of proposed resourcing of each component at the design stage of the project so that its benefits and costs for the local food security system can be pinpointed. Changes in resourcing to reduce its costs and/or improve its benefits can then, if

Table 8.2 A framework for checking the local food security impact of investment projects at the design stage

Components of investment projects	Components of local food security system					
	Mother and child health	Employment	Other income sources (e.g. land, forests, livestock)	Local costs of:		
				Food	Fuel	Water
Construction						
Land						
Labour						
Transport						
Materials, water, fuel						
Finance						
Operation						
Labour						
Transport						
Materials, water, fuel						
Finance						
Maintenance						

To use the framework: Check through the resources which each component of the project will use in its construction, operation and maintenance. If it improves a component of the local food security system put a +; otherwise a – for a negative effect and a 0 for no effect. The purpose is to indicate the benefits and costs for the local food security system of proposed resourcing arrangements for the project.

necessary, be advocated. Typical food security issues that emerge from investment projects are access of the poor to land (particularly common land), and local sourcing of labour, materials supplies and transport, which may potentially be of considerable income benefit to the local poor but which the project designers may find easier to contract in from further afield.

In the case of institutional development projects (e.g. extension services for agriculture, health and business) the food security issues are more complex since much depends on the actual functioning of the institution. Thus at the design stage the critical issues are the proposed focus of its activities (Which target group? How to reach the target group? How can they participate?), and its likely effectiveness and sustainability.

Knowing funding agencies' requirements: The routine public sector projects in most rural areas satisfy only a small fraction of what people want and are usually confined to the most basic infrastructure investment and maintenance. In remote areas, or where the public sector is poorly funded, the local investment budget may be virtually nil.

Most rural administrations never enter upon the challenge of trying to attract project funding to their areas. But there is a lot the public manager or NGO manager can do to aid the efforts of the local MP and councillors in this task.

Sources of project funds are not confined to central government: there are local communities, local, national and international NGOs, and foreign donors all working within the country. Success in attracting project funding comes from:

o building the local ability to identify and run projects well, and be seen to run them well;
o acquiring a good track record in mobilizing local community resources;
o knowing the funding agency's requirements and fulfilling them;
o developing a working relationship with funding agencies.

Foreign donor agencies and international NGOs are obviously concerned to work closely with central government. But that does not preclude local administrators communicating with them, finding out what their funding priorities are and discussing local priorities. Chapter 9 discusses further the issues in working relations between government and NGOs.

Summary

1. Finance is a problem area for local managers. They are relatively powerless in deciding how public money is spent but fully accountable for its spending. The temptation is to leave private sector financial matters well alone. But it is essential that the manager concerned with finance for the poor understands the issues and possibilities for improvement.

2. The way forward is to learn how local financial markets are functioning with regard to the savings and loans of the poor, to try to remove obstacles blocking their better functioning and to improve the management of public sector and NGO investments.
3. The suggested steps in regard to local financial markets are:
   - First, identify the local patterns of credit and savings of the poor. Two useful participative tools to aid understanding are a table of sources and uses of finance and a seasonal calendar showing the times of year at which finance is needed and the debt position of families.
   - Second, establish whether the constraints (blocks) on effective implementation of income-generating investments for the poor are financial. Use a checklist of constraints against which to check individual investments. Other possible constraints besides finance include profitability and riskiness, inputs availability, markets, land, labour, technical and management skills.
   - Third, help to improve the local finance system for the poor. Typical reasons for financial institutions being unwilling to lend to the poor include high administrative costs per loan, no attachable assets to use as security (or political difficulties in attaching assets), poor funding proposals, better loan possibilities elsewhere. Other local reasons may include language and cultural barriers to communication.

   The task for the manager is to improve communication, encourage constructive discussion of what may be a delicate local matter, and to assist understanding of the possibilities for improvement, which generally come from banks developing a more positive attitude towards reducing the obstacles in the way of their lending to small local business, and from improved organization among the poor, such as formation of savings clubs and groups to take responsibility for loans.
4. For improving public sector investments:
   - Strengthen the local projects cycle: it is usually too slow, lacks adequate participation and is hindered by poor technical skills locally in designing projects.
   - Increase local chances of attracting project funding by building the local ability to identify and run projects well; acquiring a good track record in mobilizing local community resources; knowing the funding agency's requirements and fulfilling them; developing a working relationship with funding agencies.

CHAPTER 9
Government–NGO Co-operation

Non-government organizations (NGOs) are playing an increasingly prominent part in efforts to improve food security, particularly in remote rural areas. It is essential that public sector and NGO managers understand each others' strengths and limitations, since the working relationship between government and NGOs is rarely an easy one. The focus in this chapter is on NGOs, since their rise to prominence is recent, and they are often misunderstood within government.

The nature of NGOs

NGOs exist to carry out a particular social welfare purpose, while not being a part of government. They are private organizations but not profit oriented. They may be seen as different from government or commercial firms in that they depend on voluntary action by their members, who are motivated by a moral obligation rather than political pressure or financial gain. However, the term NGO is used to describe a wide variety of voluntary organizations which differ greatly in size, objectives and style of operation. At one extreme are large, international NGOs (such as Oxfam, Save the Children Fund, Red Cross). At the other are small, local private voluntary organizations, such as irrigation groups, credit and burial associations, most of long standing, funded only by their members and existing for a specific local purpose. In between are the nationally based NGOs in aid recipient countries, some having emerged and grown from small, local associations (e.g. Proshika in Bangladesh), while some others are the creations of government itself or of donors, the 'GONGOs' and 'DONGOs' (i.e. government organized and donor organized NGOs) (Brown and Korten 1991:74).

In recent years foreign aid for social programmes has been directed increasingly towards NGOs, both through subcontracting by donors to NGOs (particularly relief programmes) and through increased direct fundraising by international NGOs. Part of the reason for donors subcontracting to NGOs is the desire for cost saving in aid administration, and the belief that NGOs can deliver programmes more effectively. But favouring NGOs as aid deliverers also fits in with the philosophy of reducing the role of the state and encouraging local organization.

NGO dilemmas

The donor view of local NGOs as a means to deliver services on a project basis, may not always be in the best interests of the NGO or the community it serves. Local NGOs which begin to rely on donor funding often find themselves becoming distanced from their community. Furthermore, the frequent assumption that NGO projects set up for service delivery should become self-supporting may be unrealistic. Some observers argue that local NGOs are often better at raising awareness of particular issues, acting as catalysts of public opinion, rather than delivering services, such as health, education or finance.

Brown and Korten (1991) suggest that those wishing to co-operate with or assist an NGO need to take great care in understanding its nature. They distinguish between NGOs which are effectively public service contractors (PSCs), delivering services on behalf of the state or donors, and those which are people's organizations (POs), lobbying around particular social issues, e.g. minority rights, environmental concerns. Assistance to people's organizations should be with gaining the skills to organize better or to carry out particular investments; delivery of local services may well not be appropriate to their basic purpose.

Governments often face a further dilemma in working with NGOs. Insecure governments, fearful that local NGOs may become a focus of opposition, often wish to control them, through licensing or putting them under co-ordinating bodies. This stifles their effectiveness. More secure and open governments give encouragement to the formation of voluntary organizations (e.g. by tax exemptions on donations).

One negative consequence of NGOs' increased popularity and support is the rising number of NGOs of dubious worth. 'Suitcase NGOs' is the vivid expression used in Uganda to describe them. To sort out the genuine from the less genuine NGOs, the 'test of voluntarism' proposed by Brown and Korten (1991:76) is useful, since NGOs are essentially voluntary organizations:

- Does the NGO have a consistent record, with a 'well defined sense of its own mission'?
- Do its staff and leaders work for it out of commitment to its mission? In particular, have they put up with adverse working conditions and less than market level salaries, where that has been necessary to fulfil the mission?
- Does it have a programme that has evolved through learning from its own experience? Good NGOs have a strong internal learning process.
- Does its programme consist mainly of the latest donor priorities (e.g. women in development one year, sustainability the next)? Good NGOs build long-term programmes with their own character.

Working with local NGOs

The most frequently found NGOs in rural areas are indigenous voluntary organizations set up to provide a specific community service which cannot be provided by an individual. The best known are the irrigation groups set up among farmers to maintain and control their irrigation systems (Curtis 1991). Others include rotating credit funds, e.g. savings clubs and burial societies; these are often women's associations or based within a local ethnic minority. Advocacy groups (e.g. defence of minority or women's rights, or environmental lobby groups) are usually of more recent origin.

The presence of such groups is a sign of a healthy community. They play a vital role in combating social ills. In the case of child care and nutrition improvement, women's groups are at the centre of the best programmes; farmers' groups are basic to the best agricultural research and extension efforts; local residents' associations are the backbone of voluntary efforts to improve community facilities, e.g. community halls, water points, clinics; parent-teacher associations are the main providers of education in many rural areas of low income countries where government-provided educational services are lacking or run down.

The challenge for the public manager is to encourage local voluntary organizations and to help combine their efforts with such services as government is able to provide locally. Perhaps the most difficult task is communicating effectively with NGOs. The temptation for the unconfident public manager working with uneducated rural people is to lecture them at public meetings (in order 'to enlighten them'). This maintains or increases distance, and does not build trust and understanding. The confident manager prefers to use participative techniques (see Appendix I) to get to know local organizations and realizes that local people are usually the best judges of local difficulties and possibilities.

Strengths and weaknesses of national and foreign NGOs

The chief strength of any voluntary organization is its devotion to a specific social cause, enabling it to command a high level of moral respect, and motivate people to contribute funds and energy. NGOs work best when very familiar with the target group, the local environment, and when they enjoy the active interest and support of local people (not only the target group) and the local media.

From the rural public manager's point of view, national and foreign NGO projects may be of particular benefit since they hold the possibility of bringing resources and committed, skilled people to the area, able to work over a long period with groups of deprived people. In short, NGOs in theory complement government development efforts excellently.

But the conditions for NGOs to perform most effectively are not always present and when they are not the actual effectiveness of an NGO can fall well below expectations. Typical problems that can reduce their effectiveness include:

- lack of familiarity with the area or the target group;
- lack of experience in working with government departments and personnel;
- empire building: where the NGO is a major resource provider locally and government is weak, it may be put into a more influential decision-making position than it should be, especially where it has no accountability to local people;
- destructive competition between rival NGOs jockeying for influence locally: this again tends to happen where government locally is particularly weak;
- diversion of NGO resources to the local elite: this is more likely to happen indirectly, for example by a local business profiting from being a monopoly supplier to an NGO programme distributing scarce inputs to a target group, e.g. livestock, fertilizers, machinery services.

Thus for the public manager in a remote area, where government is poorly resourced, attracting NGOs to the district is both a potential benefit and a matter to be approached with care.

How to get the most benefits from national and foreign NGOs:

- Try to attract the best NGOs into the area.
- Familiarize yourself with NGO projects elsewhere in your country to find out what particular NGOs are good at.
- Develop links with the national directors of good NGOs in the country: this is particularly important for a manager with very limited resources and underpaid staff, both for attracting NGOs to the district and for managing the relations between the administration and the projects.
- Accept the challenge: if the NGO project staff are good they will bring not only expertise, money and commitment but also a challenge to the local administration regarding the effectiveness of development efforts in the district. This can be positive: an incentive to the local administration to keep ahead of the issues.
- Assist their efforts: co-ordination (a much abused and unpopular word!) is not about interference; it is about communicating and encouraging. NGO staff are often zealous and competitive with each other. They work best when running their own separate projects with a clear mission. Put together on the same project the competing ideals between staff from different NGOs may wreck it.
- Understand what NGOs find difficult about working with government: NGO staff often complain of the slowness of government, its bureaucratic procedures, favouring of local elites, lack of focused objectives,

poorly motivated or corrupt staff, and apparent lack of real concern about the humanitarian issues that the NGOs themselves are deeply involved with.

The practice of secondment and salary supplementation of local administrative staff to foreign NGOs is widespread in the poorest countries but indicates a deep malaise in the civil service of those countries. Inevitably it reduces the authority of the local administration as the NGO holds the purse strings. This poses a two-way challenge: for the local government manager, who may see a foreign based organization enjoying more influence locally than it should, and some of his or her best local staff drawn away to the NGO at much increased pay; and for the local manager of the NGO, who may be tempted to use this influence. This is an internal problem within the civil service, which is not resolvable in the short term, and which raises a problem of local decision-making power. The way forward on the latter is through strengthening the local democratic institutions, all too often very weak in remote areas. The greater the extent to which executives, whether in the administration or in NGOs, are openly accountable to the elected local leadership and the community, the more does decision-making power lie where it should. Therefore commitment to supporting and strengthening the democratic effectiveness of the local council is the essential counterbalance to executive power, whether exercised by government or NGOs.

NGOs and food security

In the public image, the best known food security role of NGOs is emergency food distribution. But this is not the image that most NGOs wish to have in food security improvement. Though all recognize that it is essential to participate in emergency relief, many (Oxfam particularly) are explicit in recognizing that the benefits of food aid are confined to emergency relief and that little strengthening of institutional capacity for future famine prevention may come out of an emergency relief effort where government continues to be weak. The experience of Kordofan Province, Sudan, in the great drought of 1984–6 provides an example. CARE virtually ran the relief effort, acting on contract from the US government which provided the food aid. But this was a last resort in an emergency; there was no continuing NGO involvement, and, given the continuingly low government capacity, little 'institutional learning' from the effort. In general, NGOs are best placed to assist with famine prevention in districts where they are already running projects in their field of expertise over the medium to long term. They are then familiar with local conditions, their projects are on stream, and the projects can be expanded to accommodate the greater need in times of stress.

The drought relief effort in Kenya in 1984–5 illustrates co-operation between government and NGOs, both local and foreign, in a food emergency (Downing, Gitu and Kamau 1989). Again, CARE acted on behalf of the US government, supplying food aid to NGOs. The government of Kenya invited NGOs to help in moving imported relief supplies to affected areas and assisting the districts with distribution. NGOs' transport costs were also covered by the CARE programme. The Kenya National Council for Social Services (KNCSS) co-ordinated the NGOs' efforts. In northern districts NGOs (World Food Programme, Oxfam, World Vision, Unesco, some Catholic missions) ran innovative restocking projects (see Chapter 7). Others expanded school feeding, mother and child programmes, food for work, mobile clinics and food distribution. Action Aid and Plan International provided funds for schools, which suffered in the drought from declining income as parents in low rainfall areas were unable to pay school fees.

The ongoing contribution of NGOs, not only in times of stress, is through their programmes in health, women's education, nutrition, water, skills and income generation. Numerous NGOs work in these fields; many are large and general in their concern (e.g. World Vision, Oxfam) but most are much smaller and more specifically focused on a particular vulnerable group (e.g. Age Concern) or a particular sector (e.g. Water Aid). Many have a religious basis (e.g. Christian Aid). Many larger NGOs are linked into the international aid funding network, consisting of the national aid agencies of donor countries, the multilateral donors (e.g. World Bank, EU) and the UN agencies (e.g. Unicef, FAO, WHO, ILO), through carrying out projects funded by them. But by far the largest part of funding for most NGOs comes from direct donations from sympathetic members of the public and private companies.

Summary

1. NGOs are different from government or commercial firms in that they depend on voluntary action by their members. The term NGO covers a wide variety of voluntary organizations which differ greatly in size, objectives and style of operation.
2. In recent years foreign aid for social programmes has been directed increasingly towards NGOs. But using local NGOs as a means to deliver services on a project basis, may not always be in the best interests of the NGO or the community it serves. Local NGOs are often better at raising awareness of particular issues and acting as catalysts of public opinion than delivering services.
3. The frequent assumption that NGO projects set up for service delivery should become self-supporting may be unrealistic.
4. Secure and open governments give encouragement to the formation of genuine voluntary organizations (e.g. by tax exemptions on donations).

To sort out the genuine from the less genuine NGOs, the 'test of voluntarism' proposed by Brown and Korten (1991:76) may be applied: whether the NGO has a consistent record of learning from its own experience, whether it commands substantial voluntary effort from its staff, and whether it has evolved its own priorities.

5. The presence of active local voluntary groups is a sign of a healthy community. The challenge for the rural administrator is to encourage them and to help combine their efforts with such services as government is able to provide locally.
6. NGOs work best when very familiar with the target group, the local environment, and when they enjoy the active interest and support of local people (not only the target group) and the local media.
7. Problems sometimes encountered with NGOs beginning work in a local area include lack of local familiarity, empire building, destructive competition between rival NGOs and diversion of NGO resources to a local elite.

CHAPTER 10
Preparedness for Famine Prevention

'Careers of local administrators and politicians are made or broken in times of scarcity'.
Senior Administrator, India

The local administrator or manager who is personally poorly equipped to deal with disasters is instantly recognizable: he or she is a poor communicator and poorly connected to people and organizations that matter in promoting development and preventing famine, who waits for orders from the centre, who communicates only with his or her direct superior in regional or central government, and who does not build up own contacts with local and national politicians, with national and foreign NGOs, with donor representatives, with journalists – local, national and foreign. Above all, he or she is afraid to take a high profile position, from which stems a lack of confidence to communicate and investigate.

There is an institutional learning curve in famine prevention, relief and rehabilitation. The experiences of recent decades, and the increased involvement of donors (USAID prominently), specialist multilateral organizations (FAO and WFP particularly) and NGOs, have brought improvements in the organization of relief and rehabilitation in virtually all countries at risk: in the handling of increased quantities of emergency food aid, in provision for early warning of disaster and in institutional arrangements for managing government relief efforts and co-ordination with international organizations. Among the documented examples of achievements and improvements in disaster administration are India, Bangladesh, Botswana, Kenya and Zimbabwe (Dreze and Sen 1989; Curtis, Hubbard and Shepherd 1988; Downing, Gitu and Kamau 1989).

However, the improvements have been mainly at the central level: in national early warning systems, and particularly in the receipt, handling, storage and distribution of food aid. In many countries, despite the improvements at central level, the task is yet to be confronted of building the capacity at local level to prevent collapse of incomes and large-scale loss of assets following natural or civil disasters. They are still at the most basic stage of famine prevention, namely, trying to ensure that sufficient food is available nationally and that there is the capacity to distribute it. In the most war-disrupted countries (e.g. Somalia, Sudan) institutional improvements made in the 1970s and 1980s for relief and rehabilitation have been undermined.

Together with local political leaders, the rural manager in a high risk area faces a great challenge and responsibility in famine prevention, particularly where support from the national level is weak. The challenge is to:

- Bring people and resources together early enough when disaster threatens.
- Create self-targeting income support activities as far as possible, i.e. those which attract only those most in need.
- Get the interest and commitment from people and organizations to set up preparedness arrangements.
- Encourage community institutions through which people can effectively express their needs, particularly in times of stress.

For famine prevention, local people are dependent on the administration, to a greater extent even than local politicians (particularly where they are uneducated), as their main means of contact with the rest of the world, not only with national government. At the most basic, irreducible level, the administrator is the person with the telephone or radio.

In sum, it is now clear from many countries' experience that famine can be prevented by local action supported by central action in all but intensive war situations. The aim of this chapter is to provide guidelines for local preparedness plans. It first suggests the basic policy and managerial orientation necessary for successful disaster prevention, then provides an annotated checklist of essential disaster preparedness measures, and finally identifies priorities for local preparedness administration under adverse circumstances. A local preparedness plan for a high drought risk area (Turkana, northern Kenya) is summarized in Appendix II.

The basis for disaster preparedness

Underlying successful disaster prevention measures is an orientation of policy and administration towards:

Building a strong network of communication

Disaster relief and rehabilitation requires co-ordinated action, for which information is the basis and communication the means, both within the local area and at the national and international level. Communication is not simply a matter of telephones, radios, roads and transport, but also of who to contact and expect co-operation from, in local communities, in regional and central government, with NGOs, donors, and the press.

Reducing chronic food insecurity

The most effective insurance against famine is a wealthy and healthy population. Measures which reduce chronic (i.e. long-term) food insecurity increase the ability of people to withstand disaster both because they improve their health and protect their incomes and because ongoing programmes provide the basis from which to expand quickly in times of great need.

Policies to reduce chronic food insecurity act directly through nutrition, health and sanitation, income raising, improving food markets and investments which make production and incomes less vulnerable to disaster (improving water catchment and control, introducing drought/flood-resistant crop and tree species, increased alternative income sources in secondary and tertiary activities).

The weaker the action to reduce chronic food insecurity the greater the disaster risk and the more effective disaster preparedness needs to be. It is no surprise that those countries with the greatest chronic food insecurity need the best disaster preparedness.

Reinforcing people's own means of coping (their 'coping strategies')
Government emergency action can never supply more than a small fraction of people's needs; therefore it should always be directed to supplementing people's own efforts to cope, provided these do not destroy the environment. Coping strategies include cropping diversity, livestock movement, increased use of common resources such as forests and fisheries, and migrant labour by employable household members. These 'fall-back options' vary locally and ways of supporting them need to be investigated and discussed participatively.

Forests, wild animals and fisheries suffer particularly during times of scarcity because desperate people increase their use of common resources greatly, through cutting trees for sale as firewood or charcoal and hunting and fishing more intensively. Building up forestry reserves and allowing them to be used more heavily in times of scarcity is a preparedness strategy that has been pursued in India. But local communities are now being invited increasingly to participate in managing formerly government administered 'reserves' of forests, fisheries and wildlife, in an effort both to preserve them (since local people themselves then lose from overuse) and to enable local people to benefit more from them (Harrison 1987).

Seasonally based action
Drought and floods are seasonal in nature. In countries which suffer periodic severe drought or floods, some drought or flooding is likely in some areas, to some degree, each year. The key to effective action to combat disasters is a regular seasonal cycle of preparedness since this:

○ puts the preparedness apparatus into gear smoothly on a routine basis each year;

- can reduce long-term disaster vulnerability, since progress can be made each year with improving essential infrastructure (e.g. by drought-proofing and flood-proofing) through seasonal public works;
- deals with localized stress (e.g. localized droughts or floods) and prevents the build-up of stress from one year to another.

Targeted action
It goes without saying that the limited resources available for assistance provide the greatest benefit when directed to those most in need. A policy and managerial orientation to targeting resources to the needy is developed only with sustained effort (to alter the institutional culture of the administration in this direction) and with substantial participation by local communities in targeting decisions.

Essential disaster preparedness measures: national and local

This section overviews essential disaster preparedness measures needed at both national and local level, presenting them in the form of annotated checklists. Its purpose is to enable a comparison to be made between present arrangements and what is required in food security planning, to see what improvements remain to be made.[1]

1. Establish a clear authority structure and institutional capability for planning and organizing relief programmes, with assignment of overall and detailed responsibility at different levels of government.
Most countries vulnerable to drought or floods have established an institutional framework for:

- assembling information on food stocks, imports and food aid requirements and receiving information on need from different parts of the country;
- co-ordinating central contributions of finance and personnel and releasing them;
- receiving and storing food aid, and distributing it to where it is needed.

These functions are usually taken on by interministerial drought committees, chaired by the finance ministry, with the responsibility for receiving, storing and dispatching food aid given to a department created for the purpose (as in the Relief and Rehabilitation Commission in Ethiopia and Sudan, and the Food Resources Department in Botswana), or to the Grain Marketing Board (as in Zimbabwe). Grain marketing boards play a major role in distribution of grain and attempts to stabilize food markets.

Differences, and weaknesses, are greater in the organization at the local level. In the better managed Indian states, including Gujarat and

Maharashtra, drought preparedness has been taken to the most detailed administrative levels, with the 'Scarcity Manual' coming into operation once drought is declared in a district. The manual specifies the tasks of each type of local officer in combating the drought, and gives special authority to the district administrator (collector) to command the resources of line departments. At the opposite extreme are countries (e.g. Sudan, Somalia) which have virtually no capacity at local level, due to the disruption of the local administration by war or their virtual lack of resources. Drought relief efforts thus tend to be handed over to foreign NGOs (e.g. CARE, Save the Children) and effectively consist only of food distribution, with too little co-operation between the national level structures, the line departments and local government. In between these two extremes are systems which rely on the strength of the local administration, in co-operation with central relief institutions, to be able to deal with relief without detailed drought preparedness regulations. Kenya, Zimbabwe and Botswana fall into this category.

Whichever the system, it is clear that creating central co-ordinating institutions, while it improves the famine prevention system considerably, does not substitute for effective local administration without which the system as a whole cannot work well.

2. Establish early warning and monitoring systems for high risk areas.

The most effective early warning of impending hardship is expressed by people themselves, where there are active community institutions, political representatives and a vigorous local and national press. But these conditions are far from present in most populations at risk, which is the reason for increased emphasis on national and local drought early warning systems, monitoring rainfall and using remote sensing (air surveys, satellite imagery), in the most famine vulnerable regions. The Horn of Africa (see Box 10.1) illustrates an extreme case of the advantages and limitations of early warning systems under adverse circumstances.

In less extreme situations and wherever public action relies upon administrative initiative to a high degree, an information system is essential, to make known the likely location and extent of shortfalls in income and/or food and provide the basis for targeting.

Thus in Gujarat state, India, each June the state government sets up a monsoon monitoring office to receive daily rainfall reports. Together with reports from district level on crop state and welfare, and pressure from local politicians and media, these anticipate hardship at an early stage (Curtis, Hubbard and Shepherd 1988:120).

A well functioning early warning system is not one-dimensional (e.g. remote sensing only) nor should it produce information only for the administration, as Dreze and Sen warn (1989:84). It is part of an information system designed to alert media, politicians and government, and to

> **Box 10.1** *Early warning by remote sensing: The Horn of Africa*
>
> The Horn of Africa, in recent years increasingly war-ridden and famine vulnerable, provides a vivid example of the usefulness and limitations of early warning systems based on remote sensing. Sudan, Ethiopia and Somalia have established national Early Warning Systems (EWS) with the assistance of donors. In addition a regional EWS has been started by IGADD (comprising Djibouti, Ethiopia, Kenya, Somalia, Sudan and Uganda) and Sudan is a member of the USAID sponsored food early warning system for the Sahel. The result of the upsurge in EWS activity is that up to date satellite imagery is readily available for the whole region, enabling predictions of crop states. This proved particularly useful in anticipating the 1989–90 drought and need for emergency relief in Tigray and Eritrea, otherwise inaccessible because of war. With the present task being undertaken by the IGADD Early Warning and Food Information System of reconciling time series of satellite imagery and agro-economic data down to district level the basis for predicting hardship and vegetational change could improve greatly, provided local level agro-economic data is improved.
>
> But the rapid development of EWS, which are remote sensing based and donor financed and run, stands in sharp contrast to the deterioration of ground based EWS in the most at-risk areas of the region (north eastern Ethiopia, Somalia, south and western Sudan) and to the continuing inability of most of the states to make adequate use of the improved remote sensing data to prevent famine by any means other than emergency food distribution when deprivation is already advanced.

monitor the situation of the most vulnerable people and the impact of assistance. The indicators used in the information system should be selected according to the *source* of people's incomes and the degree to which people's incomes rely on *markets* (i.e. buying and selling products or selling labour). Direct indication of suffering (*nutritional status*) is appropriate in extreme situations for monitoring the impact of relief. It is not an early warning indicator. Botswana has a system of *nutritional surveillance* through village clinics (weighing all children brought to the clinic) which is used for monitoring relief impact and the state of chronic malnutrition in an area.

Categories of indicators of stress
Indicators used can be divided into three groups:

- Production:
  - decline in range condition
  - increases in livestock mortality
  - increased livestock distress and diseases related to malnutrition (e.g. calf mortality, measles)
  - fall in area cultivated
  - fall in area harvested
- Markets:
  - sharp changes in prices (grain price increases, livestock price falls, casual labour price falls)

○ People:
- increased sale of personal valuables (jewellery, spears)
- unusually large numbers of people migrating for work
- falls in nutritional status, particularly of infants, children and pregnant and nursing women using anthropometric measures:
  - upper arm circumference
  - weight for height
  - weight for age
  - height for age.

For early warning purposes, production indicators are important since they determine to a large extent the subsequent changes in market indicators and ultimately in nutrition indicators. But early warning indicators cannot be precise, nor should they be: they signal the need for investigation of likely stress in an area. For this purpose reports in the local press or from local councillors of production difficulties, unusual market or migration changes and of appeals for assistance, are the most important in remote rural areas. The follow-up investigation may wish to look at nutritional status, but it is not usually a first indicator. Buchanan-Smith and Davies (1995) and Young (1992) provide comprehensive and practical discussions of early warning.

A limitation of early warning systems is that they do not provide a clear indication of the extent of action to be taken to relieve hardship. Some indicate warning levels, as in the 'normal', 'alert', 'alarm', and 'emergency' adopted for the Turkana system (see Appendix II). Each level triggers preparedness actions in food stocks, public works and livestock markets. Another approach is taken in Gujarat state where local early warning systems emphasize rainfall levels and crop state assessments, with low levels triggering more detailed investigation of the area and preparation of a 'master plan' for relief. Ultimately action needs to be suited to the particular circumstances of the locality: there is a limit to the mechanical working of any early warning system.

3. Target assistance to where it is most required.

An adequate early warning and information system provides the information needed for focusing assistance to where it is most needed. The most basic information is population distribution: the number of people in a particular area. Next is their level of need and identifying those most in need. Thus in Kordofan region, Sudan, in the widespread drought of 1984–6, in the absence of sound information on population, effective targeting of food distribution by area proved impossible until mobile monitoring teams were organized to assess the adequacy of deliveries and continuing need.

General rules for targeting include:

○ The more widespread the need and poorer the information on population distribution, the more difficult it is to target assistance

by area or household. Monitor impact of initial assistance and adjust accordingly.
- To improve household targeting use *self-targeting* assistance: at the national level this may mean subsidizing or distributing an inferior food (i.e. a food consumed by the poor). But in practice this may be complicated by unavailablity of inferior foods in times of drought and by its diversion to stock feed. At the local level self-targeting can be used for income support by means of works employment for which households offer themselves for work if they need to earn the food or money wages. In India, 'test works' are opened in areas where it is thought that there is hardship and people may need to earn additional income.
- Ongoing programmes to reduce chronic food insecurity provide the most effective means of area and personal targeting of nutrition and income assistance during times of extreme hardship. Nutrition programmes established through clinic or school networks or on a village basis, and works programmes – preferably creating assets that reduce long-term disaster vulnerability (dams, roads, afforestation), the work on which can be expanded or reduced as required.
- Targeting of individual households within rural communities requires the community itself to identify its most deprived households, with the process of targeting being open and participative. Otherwise equal distribution of assistance among households is the only option, and is the one most usually resorted to in emergencies.

4. Establish principles and procedures governing the declaration of a food emergency in any area.

Clear procedures for putting a local relief effort into operation are required, whether or not there is a formal, prepared plan of operations. Decisions on when to open up works employment schemes, or when to begin food distribution, require prior decisions releasing funds for such purposes.

In Gujarat, the decision to declare a district drought-stricken is taken by the state government in consultation with the district collector; a district 'master plan' for combating the drought is then prepared, financed by special federal drought funds. Less formal arrangements, as in Kenya in the 1984-6 drought, do work provided there is adequate administrative capacity. But systematic preparedness would have improved the Kenyan effort: the 'skilled and extensive administrative bureaucracy facilitated the reporting of food shortages and delivery of commercial and relief food' but 'lack of a systematic preparedness plan . . . resulted in delays in food relief programs, shortcomings in making the best use of non-governmental organizations, lack of preparedness for recovering from the drought (most notably a shortage of seed), and costly excess stocks of yellow maize after the food crisis had ended' (Downing *et al.* 1989:10).

5. Finance: reserve funds or have pre-arranged lines of credit and conditional donor pledges available for raising the necessary funds for financing a major relief operation, with clear rules for release of funds.

Some states (e.g. Botswana, Ethiopia, Kenya, India) now have drought reserve funds. It is not financially sensible to maintain these at a level high enough to provide the resources needed to combat a major drought. For this purpose lines of credit and conditional pledges from donors are essential, particularly for food deficit countries facing unstable export markets. Thus Kenya in 1984 was fortunate to have had substantial foreign reserves enabling it speedily to import grain. Most of the poorest and most vulnerable countries (e.g. Horn of Africa, Sahel) have had increasing involvement of bilateral and multilateral agencies in emergency assistance; but there are still no standby emergency food supply arrangements, these still being made on an *ad hoc* basis.

6. Evaluate performance of past relief operations and improve preparedness arrangements accordingly.

Evaluations of relief programmes have been carried out by donors and by individual researchers. These evaluations have generally been only partial, often concentrating on the activities of a particular donor. Few have been commissioned by government and released publicly, as has been done in Botswana and Kenya. Preparation and continual improvement of relief manuals, covering both the national and local levels, best ensures that lessons learnt are incorporated in the famine prevention system.

7. Arrange procedures for publicity and mass media communication.

8. Establish arrangements for harnessing the energies of communities, local politicians and traditional leaders to combat the emergency.

9. Prepare an overall famine prevention strategy where this has not yet been done.

This can:

- enable the magnitude of the problem to be gauged (how large the gap is between present levels of organization and preparedness and what is necessary);
- define responsibilities in relation to famine prevention, which is the major shortcoming with present relief and preparedness arrangements;
- indicate what resources are necessary to fund the improved effort and how they can be obtained and organized;
- indicate the steps to be taken in strengthening the famine prevention system.

10. At the local level, prepare relief contingency plans and specify tasks to be undertaken and procedures to enter into force in the event of acute and large-scale shortages.

These would include:

Food

- If necessary, maintain minimum reserve stocks of essential grains at strategic locations.

Maintaining stable food markets is essential. Where transport, and communications are good, and traders can move food without hindrance, local availability of food depends mainly upon people having the money to buy it. But in remote areas with poor communications, shortages tend to develop seasonally, and prices to rise sharply. If there is drought in addition the price rise may be much sharper even, at a time when local incomes are lower. Under such circumstances where the food market does not function well there is a strong case for a strategic food reserve to be held at the regional or local level. Thus in Darfur region, in remote western Sudan, a strategic reserve was put in place in the late 1980s.

In situations where there is high risk of extreme food shortages, the preparedness plan should include contingency arrangements for the following:

- advance arrangments needed for introducing or intensifying food procurement operations;
- advance plans for the distribution of food, including co-ordination of procurement, handling, storage and distribution;
- regular collection of information on population by different categories in areas prone to food shortages with a view to estimating their food requirements during shortages and if necessary selecting zones where rationing may be introduced;
- advance arrangements for establishing feeding centres during shortages;
- an inventory of transport facilities available in the private sector which could be mobilized during a food crisis;
- identifying field agencies through which rationing could be arranged as well as rules of operation;
- ability to finalize movement of supplies before the onset of the rainy season.

Health

- Identify areas where there is any risk of disease epidemics among debilitated people, and prepare plans, personnel and equipment for preventing outbreaks of disease. This is an inevitable risk in refugee camps: contagious disease risks worsen with movement of people, crowding and poor sanitation. People do not die from starvation but from diseases to which they become highly susceptible when badly malnourished.

Income

- Prepare a shelf of labour intensive projects in each vulnerable area with as much operational detail as is feasible, and ensure that the supervision, materials, equipment and finance are available at the local level to put these projects into operation within days.

○ Establish the key fall-back income sources of people in vulnerable areas and fix standby arrangements for assisting the productive use of these (e.g. assisted migration for work, growing of famine reserve crops, reserved forest areas).

Livestock

○ Make advance provision for supporting livestock markets in drought vulnerable areas where livestock are an important asset, through fodder or grazing provision and/or through purchase or grain-livestock swap arrangements.

Water

○ Identify critical water sources for 'drought proofing' and ensure that operational capacity is locally available for improving water supplies in times of need.

Seeds

○ Ensure that adequate supplies of local seeds are available so that planting can take place after a drought and local crop genes are not unnecessarily replaced.

In general, the achievements in vulnerable countries in improving their famine prevention systems are mostly at the level of central organization of early warning and relief supplies. The continuing failure is in effective and timely response at the local rural level where, in some of the most vulnerable areas, particularly those hit by war, the famine prevention system has deteriorated along with the capacity of the local administration.

Making local preparedness management more effective under adverse circumstances

Local preparedness and response is the more difficult the greater the local food insecurity, the poorer the resources of government locally to combat it and the less interested or able central government is in providing resources.

The more adverse the circumstances the better connected and prepared to take initiative the administrator needs to be. Priorities include:

○ *Encourage long-term investments which strengthen fall-back resources of the community*, i.e. those which they rely on heavily in times of deprivation. Trees are a key fall-back resource – they are among the first to go. Thus facilitating cultivation of utility trees around homes and lands, and maintaining forestry reserves, for food, fodder and cash is critical. Improving water catchments, and ensuring that local agricultural policies

do not discourage farmers from growing reserve food crops are other essentials.
- *Press regional and central government continually for improved preparedness arrangements.* Press at multiple points: through immediate superiors and at higher levels, through the political as well as the administrative system. Be specific as to what is required – specific requests are more readily addressed than ones vaguely expressed. Appendix II summarizes the local preparedness plan for Turkana District as an illustration of what can be done under adverse circumstances.
- *Press for development projects of any kind, but particularly any which will provide additional slack season employment.* Even small development projects bring money, trained personnel and communications equipment to remote areas – all of which are essential in an emergency. In remote areas of Kordofan and Darfur provinces of Sudan in the great drought of 1984–6 it was the areas with development projects which were able provide nuclei for relief activity.
- *Build own connections with NGOs and with local and national press.* Exceptional circumstances call for exceptional measures; in an impending emergency a local manager must not rely only on those further up the administrative hierarchy to communicate with those who can provide or encourage assistance.
- *Think participatively: the energies and creativity of the people likely to be most adversely affected are the most valuable resource.*

APPENDIX I
Rapid and Participatory Appraisal Tools

Rapid rural appraisal (RRA) emerged in the late 1970s as a result of dissatisfaction with time consuming questionnaire-based surveys as a means of gathering information for assessing policy-related issues in rural communities, and from dissatisfaction with 'rural development tourism', i.e. superficial visits to rural areas by policymakers and funders. The goal was fast but accurate learning. Based on a philosophy of 'optimal ignorance' (you don't need to learn everything) it focused on improving interview techniques (using 'key informants', semi-structured interviews with checklists, 'triangulating', i.e. using additional sources to check information). Because it attempted to fill so important a need it attracted much interest and has benefited greatly from a spirit of open, co-operative enquiry in exchanging information on new techniques experimented with. The result is a long menu of techniques based on interviewing and practical exercises, to which additions are continually being made.

By the early 1990s the emphasis had shifted towards participative rural appraisal (PRA), in order to move beyond RRA's concern with extracting information, towards an approach in which the informants themselves participate more in the gathering and the use of the information. In PRA the outsider becomes facilitator as much as investigator, the information is 'owned, analysed and used by local people' (Chambers 1992:13); the focus is less on information for government or NGO policy than on community action; the philosophy has shifted towards the process of participative enquiry itself. RRA and PRA are used in agricultural planning, natural resource management, poverty alleviation programmes, health and food security promotion (e.g. Maxwell 1989; Buchanan-Smith 1992). They can also be used for analysing institutions. The stress of PRA is on using your own initiative and creativity in adopting and adapting methods appropriate to the task.

The advantages of RRA and PRA are cost-effectiveness, building close working relationships with communities and a high level of reliability of the information generated. One disadvantage is that, if done badly, they can give false legitimacy to sloppy field investigations; but in this they are no more open to abuse than are survey methods. As in all investigations, the test is the reliability of the information, and the quality of the insights gained. To these, participatory appraisal carried out well adds improved confidence acquired by the community and by the investigator in discussing the issue in question.

The following is a summary list, adapted from Robert Chambers' overview of PRA and RRA approaches and techniques (1992:16–18):

- *key informants:* enquiring who are the experts and seeking them out;
- *semi-structured interviews:* regarded by some as the 'core' of good RRA; usually uses checklists of issues and key visual objects around which to base discussion (e.g. seed types, pest types, aerial photographs, models);
- *groups:* specialist, neighbourhood, community group interviews;
- *scoring and ranking:* using matrices to allocate scores to different trees, soils, etc. for different qualities such as hardiness, fertility;
- *participatory mapping, modelling:* people make maps, models and diagrams of social, demographic, health and natural resource characteristics; or construct three-dimensional models of their farms or village;
- *participatory diagramming:* of flows, causes, amounts, trends, rankings, scorings – in which people make their own diagrams, matrices, bar diagrams, pie charts, and Venn diagrams (*'Chapati'*) to identify the relationships among individuals and institutions important in and for a community;
- *wealth or well-being ranking:* using cards with household names on them, informants rank and group the cards according to households' perceived wealth or well-being, in order to identify those considered best or worst off;
- *transect walks:* 'systematically walking through an area, or along a water course, observing, asking, listening, discussing, identifying different zones, local technologies, introduced technologies, seeking problems, solutions and opportunities, and mapping and diagramming';
- *seasonal diagramming:* of seasons or months of the year indicating days and amounts of rain or soil moisture, crops, agricultural and non-agricultural labour, diet, diseases, fodder, migration, income, expenditure, debt, etc.;
- *time lines:* chronologies of the main events in a household or village's history, e.g. in order to locate dates of particular times of stress, such as drought, floods;
- *trend lines:* indicating trends of change, e.g. in land use, cropping patterns, ecological features, settlement, migration, fuels, customs, education, health, finance, etc.;
- *estimates and quantification:* 'often using local measures, judgements, and materials such as seeds, pellets, fruits or stones as counters, sometimes combined with maps or models';
- *home visits:* where not intrusive, home visits to the poor often provide more solid discussions of real problems and means of coping than if conducted away from the home.

Sources of information on RRA and PRA: The key source is *RRA Notes*, issued by the Institute for International Development (IIED). Contact: RRA Notes, IIED, 3 Endsleigh Street, London, WC1H 0DD. Phone: 0171-388 2117. Fax: 0171-388 2826.

APPENDIX II
Kenya's Turkana District drought preparedness plan

Turkana District lies in arid north-west Kenya around Lake Turkana. Livestock and fishing are principal sources of livelihood. A drought preparedness plan has been drawn up. Its objectives are summarized below, adapted from Swift (1989).

In the event of a major drought:

(a) To encourage substantial but orderly stock reduction, while maintaining the purchasing power of herders, avoiding massive animal deaths, and maintaining a reservoir of breeding females for later restocking.
(b) To maintain adequate supplies of cereals at controlled prices, at shops spread widely across the district.
(c) To maintain, as far as possible, a dispersed pattern of population distribution, and to avoid the creation of large famine-relief camps with their public health dangers.
(d) To provide employment on useful works to destitute people.
(e) To guarantee a minimum of emergency feeding and health care to vulnerable people.
(f) To ensure that the drought preparedness measures are implemented, including an early warning system and cereal reserves, to ensure that the district administration has the ability to prevent drought turning into famine by early reaction.

Policy to achieve these objectives:

1. Providing the extra staff and funds needed

○ A special district drought contingency fund for immediate emergency relief;
○ Pre-arranged commitments with central government and donors concerning level and type of assistance to be rendered;
○ District drought management officer to co-ordinate preventive and relief work;
○ Drought contingency manual to be prepared by drought contingency officer, in co-operation with technical departments and NGOs, to enable

the accumulated experience in drought management in the district to be available to new staff and to provide clear instructions to officers;
- Standby powers for the DC to be able to commandeer staff from line departments, and vehicles, both from within government and from NGOs and the private sector;
- Standby powers to impose or free restrictions on movement of grain.

2. Physical infrastructure

- Grain storage: district strategic reserve with six months storage, with standby stores at division and location levels, and in the herder associations;
- Roads: improving the most critical roads;
- Water: improvement in water reliability (number of sources, maintenance) to ensure availability in times of stress, in:
  - population centres, especially where people are likely to gather in times of drought, to assist in maintaining adequate hygiene;
  - livestock holding camps.

3. Livestock

- Improving reserve forage requirements (i.e. holding grounds, forests, fodder tree cultivation at water sources by individuals and associations);
- Purchase campaign by the district during a drought: holding grounds, separation of stock into three parts – breeding core (to be kept in the holding grounds), weak stock (to be slaughtered locally) and those to be removed for abattoir slaughter;
- Attention to quarantine regulations: either temporarily lifting them, or arranging the slaughter and transport according to regulations;
- Funds for purchase and holding of livestock, and for fodder purchase as required to maintain core breeding stock, and to fund the restocking programme after the drought;
- Restocking programme makes use of the kept female stock as the core of the programme, using funds to finance purchase, but thereafter operating on a revolving fund basis, with recipients providing the first female offspring as payment, to be further distributed.

4. Employment

- Register of well-prepared works projects; stockpiles of tools, cadre of trained supervisors
- Possible projects include:
  - water harvesting
  - roads
  - airstrips
  - terracing
  - tree planting and husbandry, for amenity, timber, fuel, fodder

- small-scale irrigation
- check dams
○ cash payments rather than food may be easier, depending on local circumstances.

5. *Information*

○ Indicators for the early warning system and monitoring of impact of assistance: different indicators to be monitored by different departments, ongoing projects and NGOs:
  - rainfall
  - lists of destitute people receiving relief
  - cereals availability in stores, commercial and domestic
  - prices of cereals
  - unusual sales of animals, particularly females
  - range condition
  - participation in school feeding, and school attendance
  - unusual movement of people
  - increased numbers enrolled in food for work
  - nutritional status.

No single indicator is enough; the advantage of varied indicators is that more parties are involved, that the complexities of the local situation are not ignored, that monitoring is facilitated using the same indicators, and that assistance can be targeted better by area.

6. *Response*

○ Set levels (normal, alert, alarm, emergency) for indicators beyond which action to be taken.
○ Sequence proposed for Turkana:
  - Activate emergency drought sub-committee;
  - Fill cereals stores to capacity (note: if the district is food deficit and drought will greatly reduce its capacity, e.g. by reducing herds to buy in food, then arrangements for continued supplies of food to the district will be necessary – unless alternative income source is established);
  - DC to release food to traders and projects at discretion;
  - Notify provincial and central government that district drought funds may need to be drawn on soon;
  - Alert need of food aid;
  - Alert works programme organizers and supervisors;
  - Activate stock buying programme if need indicators reach alarm stage; buy animals in good condition and spread purchases among households and areas;
  - Relief feeding of those unable to work according to the relief list;
  - Assistance with access to fall-back activities, e.g. fishing, migrant work, trekking of animals.

Glossary of food security terms

Acute food insecurity	A state of extreme food deprivation, i.e. famine.
Chronic food insecurity	A long-term condition of having too little food for a healthy and productive life.
Coping strategies	The alternative sources of income or food that a household resorts to when its usual sources fail (e.g. labour migration, extra cutting of firewood for sale, splitting the livestock herd).
Counterpart funds	Cash resulting from official local sales of programme or project food aid.
Early warning systems	Gathering and assembling information (e.g. food price movements, crop and livestock condition, changes in wages, migration) to indicate famine risk so that relief can begin quickly to prevent famine.
Exchange entitlements	People's purchasing power over commodities and services; literally the commodities and services which the market offers in exchange for the commodities and services that people have to sell.
Famine	A state of acute deprivation of food.
Famine foods	Foods to which people resort during famine, usually edible roots and berries.
Food aid	Aid in the form of food. The three types of food aid are programme food aid (direct transfers of food aid to government to sell through markets and retain the counterpart funds), project food aid (to provide the resources for development projects) and emergency food aid (to be distributed as relief).
Food insecurity	Having access to too little food for health and productiveness, or being at risk of having too little food.
Food security	Having access to sufficient food for an active and healthy life. (See household food security and national food security.)
Food self-reliance	Applied to nations which have sufficient foreign exchange to pay for all their food import

	requirements, i.e. they do not need to rely upon aid to supply their food requirements.
Food self-sufficiency	Sufficient food production in the country to supply the nation's requirements.
Food supply insecurity	Same meaning as national food insecurity. Also sometimes referred to as national aggregate food insecurity.
Household food security	Access by the household to sufficient food to provide all household members with good health and an active life. Note that a household may be food secure yet have malnourished members if some members get more and others less than their requirements. (See intrahousehold food distribution.)
Intrahousehold food distribution	The sharing of food among members of the household. If the intrahousehold (i.e. 'within the household') distribution allows some members more and some less than their needs, then some members will be malnourished even if the household as a unit is food secure. (See household food security.)
Malnutrition	Insufficient intake of nutrients to live a healthy and active life.
National food security	Sufficient access to food by the nation (either in the form of local food supplies or imports) to supply the whole nation's requirements, if the supply were to be distributed according to people's needs. In practice, many nations are food secure yet contain much chronic malnutrition, and run the risk of famine because poor people lack the purchasing power or the social entitlements (see definition) to command the food they need.
Nutrients	Substances (e.g. carbohydrates, proteins, fats, vitamins) contained in food which provide essential nourishment for the maintenance of life.
Nutrition	The process of providing or receiving nutrients.
Preparedness plan	Arrangements for immediate prevention and relief activities in the event of a famine threat.
Scarcity	Used in Indian famine prevention planning to describe a situation of food security risk.
Social entitlements	The commodities and services which people can command through their social relations (e.g. transfers from family, friends, clan, government).
Transitory food insecurity	Acute food insecurity; but rarely used now.
Undernutrition	Used interchangeably with malnutrition (see definition).

Notes

Chapter 1
1. Maxwell and Frankenberger (1992:21) discuss the different types of shocks to which food insecure households are particularly vulnerable, which include sharp falls in employment and farm production; sharp rises in food prices and disease.

Chapter 2
1. Dreze and Sen (1989) use this term to refer to the assistance that households can receive from family and neighbours.
2. The term 'area' is used to refer to the particular rural area that the rural manager is concerned with. It may be a district or some sub-unit of the district. Local food security systems may vary within an area.
3. Except where they are the result of virtual siege conditions in war (as in Bosnia in 1992–3), the worst famines in recent decades have occurred in relatively remote areas of poor countries, e.g. Sudan, Ethiopia, Bangladesh.

Chapter 3
1. Details from Paul Harrison (1987:Ch. 15), who gives a simple and clear account of the WHO/Unicef 'child survival revolution'.
2. Christina Lamb ' "Barefoot doctors" wage war on Brazil's other child killers', *Financial Times*, 24 August 1993.

Chapter 4
1. A more detailed analysis of local marketing chains needs survey and thorough case study information, i.e. more interviews, in greater depth, observation and counting at points of transaction, measurement of losses and variations in prices.
2. Although rural food prices increase when normal sources of supply are reduced, as during a drought, food supplies may flow out of rural areas to the cities or abroad, if food traders can earn more from these larger volume markets. This 'counter movement' of food has been observed in India and Africa (Dreze and Sen 1989:90–1; Curtis, Hubbard and Shepherd 1988:63). Even where market prices for food are greater in rural areas than cities, selling in cities rather than rural areas may be more attractive in terms of volumes sold, marketing costs or foreign exchange realized.

Chapter 5
1. The 'culture of poverty' is the term coined by Oscar Lewis in the 1950s to describe the way of life of the poor in South and North American cities. With the present rapid growth of urban slums the 'culture of poverty' is growing. See Lewis (1959).
2. For example, the evaluation form in the Government of India's 'Continuous Evaluation of IRDP' sample survey in 1986 simply asked recipients what their income level was in the current and past year.

Chapter 7
1. The only reference to a successful pastoral dairy project I have come across is that in Abbott and Makeham (1979:36) concerning a dairy set up north of N'Djamena which 'by providing an accessible market for milk from local cattle, lifted a whole district from a subsistence level'.

Chapter 10
1. The list of requirements is based in part on FAO (1980). The Oxfam *Field Director's Handbook* (1985, Part 8) is a further valuable source on disaster preparedness.

References

Abbott, J. (1987) *Agricultural Marketing Enterprises for the Developing World*, Cambridge University Press, Cambridge.

Abbott, J. and Makeham, J. (1979) *Agricultural Economics and Marketing in the Tropics*, Longman, London.

Alamgir, M. and Poonam, A. (1991) *Providing Food Security for All*, IT Publications, London.

Berg, A. (1987) *Malnutrition: What can be done? Lessons from World Bank experience*, Johns Hopkins, Baltimore and London.

Boehm, A. (1988) *ZOPP: An introduction to the method*, Deutsche Gesellschaft fur Technische Zusammenarbeit (GTZ), Frankfurt.

Boehm, A. (1992) *ZOPP: Training Manual*, Deutsche Gesellschaft fur Technische Zusammenarbeit (GTZ), Frankfurt.

Brown, L. and Korten, D. (1991) 'Working More Effectively with Non-Governmental Organizations', in Paul, A. and Israel, A. (eds) *Non-governmental Organizations and the World Bank*, World Bank, Washington.

Buchanan-Smith, M. (1992) *Finding Out How People Prioritise Their Food Security Problems in Chad: The challenges of RRA at national level*, mimeo, Institute of Development Studies, Falmer.

Buchanan-Smith, M., and Davies, S. (1995) *Famine Early Warning and Response: The missing link*, IT Publications, London.

Casley, D. and Kumar, K. (1987) Project Monitoring and Evaluation in Agriculture, World Bank, Washington.

Chambers, R. (1993) *Challenging the Professions: Frontiers for rural development*, IT Publications, London.

Chambers, R. (1983) *Rural Development: Putting the last first*, Longman, Harlow.

Chambers, R. (1992) *Rural Appraisal: Rapid, relaxed and participatory*, IDS Discussion Paper, 311, Institute of Development Studies, Falmer.

Clay, E. (1988) 'Assessment of Food Entitlement Interventions in South Asia', in Curtis, D. *et al. Preventing Famine: Policies and prospects for Africa*, Routledge, London.

Cornia, A. *et al.* (eds) (1987) *Adjustment with a Human Face*, Unicef, Oxford.

Curtis, D. (1991) *Beyond Government*, Macmillan, London.

Curtis, D., Hubbard, M. and Shepherd, A. (1988) *Preventing Famine: Policies and prospects for Africa*, Routledge, London.

De Waal, A. (1989) *Famine That Kills: Darfur, Sudan, 1984–5*, Clarendon, Oxford.

Downing, T., Gitu, K. and Kamau, C. (eds) (1989) *Coping with Drought in Kenya: National and local strategies*, Lynne Rienner, Boulder and London.

Dreze, J. and Sen, A. (1989) *Hunger and Public Action*, Clarendon, Oxford.

FAO (1980) Ways of Improving Preparedness to Meet Acute and Large Scale Food Shortages, (CFS WP/80/5), Rome.

Feacham, R. *et al.* (1978) *Water, Health and Development*, TRI-MED, London.

Gaude, J., Guichaua, A., Martens, B. and Miller, S. 'Rural Development and Labour-intensive Schemes: Impact studies of some pilot programmes, *International Labour Review* 26:4:423–46, ILO, Geneva.

Gordon, G. (1984) 'Important Issues for Feminist Nutrition Research – A case study from the savanna of West Africa', *IDS Bulletin* 15:1:38–44.

Government of Kenya (1979) *Child Nutrition in Rural Kenya*, Central Bureau of Statistics, Ministry of Economic Planning and Community Affairs.

Hagenbuch, W. (1958) *Social Economics*, Cambridge University Press, Cambridge.

Haggblade, S. (1982) *Rural Industrial Officer's Handbook*, Ministry of Commerce and Industry, Gaborone.

Harrison, P. (1987) *The Greening of Africa*, Penguin and Paladin, New York and London.

Heifer Project International (1986) *Environmentally Sound Small-Scale Livestock Projects: Guidelines for planning*, Codel Inc, Heifer Project International and Winrock International, New York and Arkansas.

IGADD (1990) *The Potential for Increased Trade in Cereals among IGADD Member Countries*, IGADD, Djibouti.

International Institute for Environment and Development (1991) Proceedings of Workshop February 1991 Bangalore.

Kennedy, E. and Coghill, B. (1988) 'The Commercialization of Agriculture and Household-level Food Security: The case of southwestern Kenya', *World Development* 16:9:1075–81.

Leurs, R. (1993) *A Resource Manual for Trainers and Practitioners of Participatory Rural Appraisal (PRA)*, Papers in the Administration of Development, No.49, Development Administration Group, University of Birmingham.

Lewis, O. (1959) *Five Families: Mexican case studies in the culture of poverty*, Basic Books, New York.

Longman (1990) *World Development Directory*, Longman International Reference, London.

Maxwell, S. (1989) 'Rapid Food Security Assessment: A pilot exercise in Sudan', *RRA Notes* 5, International Institute for Environment and Development, London.

Maxwell, S. and Frankenberger, T. (1992) 'Household Food Security: Concepts, indicators, measurements', Unicef and IFAD.

Maxwell, S., Swift, J. and Buchanan-Smith, M. (1990) 'Is Food Security Targeting Possible in Sub-Saharan Africa? Evidence from North Sudan', *IDS Bulletin* 21:3, July, Institute of Development Studies, Brighton.

ODA (1985) *Manual for the Appraisal of Rural Water Supplies*, HMSO, London.

OECD (undated) *Directory of Non-Governmental Environmental and Development Organizations in OECD member countries: 'Environment and development in the Third World*, OECD Development Centre, Paris.

Oxfam (1985) *The Field Director's Handbook: An Oxfam manual for development workers*, Oxford University Press, Oxford.

Padmanabhan, K. (1988) *Rural Credit: Lessons for rural bankers and policy makers*, IT Publications, London.

Remenyi, J. (1991) *Where Credit is Due: Income generating programmes for the poor in developing countries*, IT Publications, London.

Sandford, S. (1983) *Management of Pastoral Development in the Third World*, Wiley, Chichester.

Sen, A. (1981) *Poverty and Famines*, Clarendon, Oxford.

Sikana, P., Kerven, C. and Behnke, R. (1993) 'From Subsistence to Specialised Commodity Production: Commercialisation and pastoral dairying in Africa'. *Pastoral Development Network* Paper 34d, Overseas Development Institute, London.

Singh, I. (1990) *The Great Ascent: The rural poor in South Asia.* Published for the World Bank. Johns Hopkins University Press, Baltimore.

Swift, J. (1989) 'Planning Against Drought and Famine in Turkana: A district contingency plan', in Downing, T. *et al.* (eds) *Coping With Drought in Kenya: National and local strategies*, Lynne Reinner, Boulder and London.

Timmer, C., Falcon, W. and Pearson, S. (1983) *Food Policy Analysis*, Johns Hopkins University Press, Baltimore.

Unicef (1989) *Improving Child Health and Nutrition: The joint WHO/Unicef nutrition support programme in Iringa, Tanzania*, Unicef, Dar es Salaam.

Unicef (1990) *Summary Report of the Iringa Nutrition Programme (INP)*, prepared for government/Unicef officials visiting Iringa region 10–14/9/90.

Unicef (1992) *State of the World's Children.*

Von Braun, J. and Pandya-Lorch, R. (1992) *Income Sources and Diversification Strategies of the Malnourished Rural Poor*, International Food Policy Research Institute, Reprint No. 250, Washington.

Von Braun, J., Teklu, T. and Webb, P. (1991) *Labor-Intensive Public Works for Food Security: Experience in Africa*, International Food Policy Research Institute, Washington.

Wallis, M. (1989) *Bureaucracy: Its role in third world development*, Macmillan, London.

Walshe, M. *et al.* (1991) *Dairy Development in Sub-Saharan Africa: A study of issues and options*, World Bank Technical Paper No. 135, World Bank, Washington.

Webb, P. and Von Braun, J. (1990) *Drought and Food Shortages in Ethiopia: A preliminary review of effects and policy implications*, International Food Policy Research Institute, Washington.

Werner, D. (1980) *Where There is No Doctor: A village health care handbook*, Macmillan, London.

Wood, G. and Palmer-Jones, R. (1991) *The Water Sellers*, IT Publications, London.

World Bank (1986) *Poverty and Hunger: Issues and options for food security in developing countries*, World Bank, Washington.

World Bank (1992) *Health in Development*, World Bank, Washington.

Young, H. (1992) *Food Scarcity and Famine: Assessment and response*, Oxfam Practical Health Guide No. 7, Oxfam, Oxford.